Fredri..
There is Great..
in You,

LK 17:21

Yakinee Marie

9/2013

The Book "The Strength of A Woman" is a timely release for healing, deliverance, and empowerment for Women from all walks of life. Yakinea Marie has endured all the challenges she speaks of in this book and by the grace of God has been transformed, and now through her own transformation it will bring about transformation in the lives of others. This is a must read for Women all over the world! Women will embrace their God given worth, reach for their goals, began to dream again, pursue their purpose, realize untapped potential and hidden talents that will impact their lives and the lives of others.

~ Pastor Lestine N. Bell
Lestine Bell Inc. & Lets Go Inc.

I absolutely loved this book. The Strength of a Woman by Yakinea Marie is truly inspiring and is an important read for every woman who is on the journey of life, pursuing her destiny. The Strength of a Woman powerfully challenges us to tap into the hidden reservoir of our God given potential. This book will ignite and transform the way you think and see yourself.

~Mama Harriett Panchoo
Mama Harriett's Mission Kitchen

To my friend, Yakinea Marie, it was with great expectation that we anticipated the release of your Expanded Edition "The Strength of a Woman". God has truly graced you with the uncanny ability to share your past and present experiences in such a way that men and women of all walks of life can relate.

~Ralph Sanders
Magic City Properties

THE STRENGTH OF A WOMAN

Born to Turn Pain into Power
(Expanded Edition – Includes Journal)

Yakinea Marie

THE STRENGTH OF A WOMAN

Copyright © 2013 Yakinea Marie Duff
All rights reserved.
ISBN 13: 978-1492267249

KEi Publishing
1710 – 2nd Avenue N, Ste 209
Birmingham, AL 35203

All rights reserved. No part of this publication may be reproduced for the purpose of financial gain. Brief quotations may be copied and used for the purpose of personal and organizational study and encouragement without the prior permission of the publisher. Upon request permission will be given.

Unless otherwise indicated, Scripture quotations are taken from the New King James Version. Copyright © 1982 by Thomas Nelson, Inc. Used by permission. All rights reserved.

For more information on upcoming events, speaking engagements, or life coaching visit:
www.TheStrengthOfaWoman.com
www.LadiesofRoyalty.com
www.YakineaMarie.com

Contents

Acknowledgment	9
Introduction	13
1) I Am Woman – Tailored For Success	17
2) The Enemy To Your Success	29
3) Where is Your Trust?	45
4) Poised For Purpose - Why Not You?	57
5) Pain Will Paralyze Your Purpose	71
6) Possess Your Power	83
7) Average Just Won't Do	95
8) You Are a Woman of Wealth	107
9) Turn Your Passion into Profit	119
10) Testimony – A Woman Who Overcame	129
11) Fall In Love With Yourself	143
Notes	151
Stay Connected	153

Acknowledgement

    I am humbled by the Lord God's faithfulness towards me. Without Him I would not know my purpose for existing or the essence of who I am; it is because of Him I am a woman in pursuit of purpose.

    In the process of life, through challenges and victories, God blesses us with a select group of people who bring with them the encouragement, love, prayers, integrity, accountability, and guidance needed to pull on the gifts and potential of the woman that lies dormant within the little girl. To the women of purpose who God has blessed me to have had the great privilege of encountering in some capacity of life I thank you.

    I am forever grateful to have had the opportunity of being able to love such a phenomenal woman; to my belated mother, Pothina Yakinea Crawford, she epitomized the strength of a woman. She did not know everything but she knew some things and those words of wisdom planted the seeds of determination and fortitude in me to never give up on my dreams. Thanks to my aunt Veronica Cook who stood as a pillar of strength to my siblings and I after my mother's passing.

    Over the years I have developed into a woman of strength and I contribute that to these great women and men of purpose: My handsome son, Jakim Jackson, who continuously reminds me of how gifted I am. My sister, Marnesha Zinnerman and my two brothers Alcarlos Reaves and Joel Crawford, their love is priceless. Daddy Joseph and Mama Harriett Panchoo, my god-parents, are phenomenal examples of love; I am grateful for their prayers, encouragement, support, and inspiration which pushed me into the next dimension of my purpose. To Soheila and Jason McKay, Rickie and Debbie Jenkins, Latonya Seals, NaKisha Cook, Tanya Suzzette Pettway, Corey Swanson, Keenya Kelly Griffin, and Eunice Long, who utilized their gifts to assist me in business and ministry. I am grateful to Kim Mason for her support through my wilderness period. Thanks to Marc Carson, Greg Thurman, and Ricardo Archbold for their motivation and encouragement.

God will always send you someone to walk with you. Thanks to Thirley Ross for her faithfulness to walk with me in ministry for over three years as my co-host. Bless you greatly!

I have overcome many obstacles that attempted to detour or destroy me. I am grateful to those who God used to develop my walk in the Word and as a lifestyle. Thank you to my former Pastor Johnnie Johnson who God led to draw me from a world of destruction into the word of growth. To Pastor Michael D. and Kennetha Moore, my spiritual mother and father at Faith Chapel Christian Center, who imparts into me wisdom and life through God's word and for living the life you teach. To Pastor Lestine Bell, a spiritual mentor, God has utilized the anointing and gifts on her life to assist me with developing into the women I am today. To Jacqueline Battle, her gift of encouragement constantly reminds me of my wealthy place as a kingdom business woman in the earth. To Pastor Theodore and Gwen Lewis for embracing me as a daughter and speaking words of life over my destiny. To Dr. Nasir Siddiki, for being the kingdom example of what a kingdom entrepreneur exemplifies. To Pastors Reginald and Brandy Gibson who have given me an international vision because of their example as Kingdom leaders.

I have been privileged to have had some wonderful business mentors. Thanks to Michael Humes, Jil Jordan Greene, Donald Bradley and Ralph Sanders for their coaching and the seeds of wisdom they planted within me. Their encouragement, constructive criticism, systems, and business strategies added to the chapter of my life.

Lastly, I am grateful to the countless men and women, whom God has used in some capacity to push, motivate, teach, inspire, and stretch my imagination. May God exceed your expectations and increase you abundantly for playing a part in the book of my life.

Introduction

The woman, although often undervalued and poorly stewarded, is a priceless piece of art, carefully designed and strategically tailored for a purpose. She is looked upon as the weaker vessel but yet possesses the internal strength and tenacity to carry the greatest of challenges simultaneously. God, her creator, did not make a mistake when He fashioned her in His image; He was indeed purposeful when He titled her the "Help Meet" because she would help meet needs where voidance exists. Who is she? She is poised, positioned, and postured for success where average just will not do. She is a woman who has been given the fortitude to turn her pain into power and her passion into profits. She is a woman of wealth; one who has embraced all that she is despite limitations. Wealth is often limited to the assets that one has accumulated or the amount of money one has acquired but true wealth is fruitful progression in every aspect of life: Emotionally, Spiritually, Relationally, Physically, and Financially. Who is she? This woman is YOU, a woman in pursuit of purpose.

Our purpose as a woman is the essence of who we are. There are many enemies who will threaten to hinder and possibly abort the seed of potential that lie internally within us, but we must intentionally push through the pain and take possession of our purpose. We, as women, have been internally empowered to shift atmospheres and move obstacles out of our lives that threaten to plant themselves as mountains. To possess the inner strength to move mountains but lack the motivation to utilize it is due to a lack of discovery of one's true power. **Pain paralyzes, void of identity causes confusion, and rejecting our personal strengths causes acceptance of weaknesses that we were created to dominate.**

All of us have overcome something whether during our childhood or as an adult, and the mere fact that we are still living, not just surviving, is a testimony. My mom, who is deceased, faced many test, trials, and pains; despite it all she was a woman of strength. I was raised in a home where drugs were prevalent due to my mother's addiction to cocaine. Whereas my three siblings and I lacked in many areas as children, my mom still found the strength in the cloudiness of her addiction to discipline us, require good grades from school, and feed us on the smallest of meals. We eventually were removed from our home and placed in foster care, later a group home for more than three years. I later learned that her addiction and inability to provide a nurturing environment for her children did not diminish her intrinsic value. My mother's traumatizing experience of losing her children gave her the motivation and strength to quit drugs without ever attending a drug rehabilitation center. She fought the courts and later received full custody of my siblings and I. Was it will power alone? Absolutely not, it was the strength that had previously been imbedded within her DNA by her designer and creator the Almighty God.

    The inspiration behind "The Strength of a Woman" transpired after witnessing and personally experiencing the struggles and strengths that we as women encounter throughout our daily lives. Once we understood and accepted the truth that we are weak, inner strength was released that only comes from God. We were reminded that God's strength is made perfect in our weakness therefore our greatest area of weakness is His greatest area of strength. Sadly enough there are ladies of royalty who have yet to discover their true worth, purpose, and intrinsic value. They have allowed themselves to succumb to the scraps of life when their King has prepared a royal table of abundance for them to feast from.

    Past abuses, pains, and even prestige or opulence does not equate to who we truly are. The potential to affect change and impact lives is within every woman regardless of her past or present insecurities, esteem level, or status.

    The enemy, which comes in many forms, desires to steal your peace and rob you of your influence. We as women of purpose, we as leaders must use the influences that have been grafted within us to build up versus tear down. We were born to operate from a place of dominion and rulership; we must take responsibility for ourselves.

The woman was created on purpose for a specific purpose. Knowing who we are as a woman gives us the courage to ignore and even reject all who would attempt to threaten the essence of our existence, including ourselves. Knowing who we are and the purpose of our existence motivates us into not compromising or lowering our standards to appeal to others. Knowing who we are propels us into action, giving us the determination and perseverance to walk over every obstacle that would attempt to stand in our way. We must know who we are; our true identity, which comes in two ways: 1) identifying ourselves by who we are in Christ 2) identifying ourselves through our purpose of why God created us. The strength of a woman is intentional. As you continue to read and journal through each chapter may your heart and mind be enlightened to truths that will propel you to move higher in your God designed purpose intentionally.

ONE

I Am Woman
Tailored for Success

> IT IS GOD WHO ARMS ME WITH STRENGTH,
> AND MAKE MY WAY PERFECT.
> ~Psalm 18:32

"It's a girl" the doctor declared loudly!!! "PURPOSE has been born!" From the moment woman was created, fashioned, and tailored she was destined to give birth to something great. She was not created to fill space, she was not fashioned to be used as a doormat, and she was not tailored to fit into the world's ideology of what she should be. Woman was strategically designed to assist in helping man birth forth purpose as she walks in her own. God said, "It is not good that man should be alone; I will make a *Help Meet* for Him."

Many titles have been given to the woman to identity the essence of who she really is, some good others bad, but the first title given to woman was "Help Meet." Other translations of the bible title her as "Help Mate" or "Helper," but she was specifically tailored to bring wholeness to an area that lacked. A "Help Meet" is simply one who assists with or helps to meet a particular need. For example: a wife helps a husband meet the need of walking in the fullness of their vision as a family by assisting, affirming, praying for, and encouraging him through the process. You, as the woman, have been purposely fashioned to help solve a problem here in the earth, and you do not have to be married first before you begin your quest toward walking in the reality of who you really are.

You, as the woman, have been purposely fashioned to help solve a problem here in the earth.

Carrying the assignment as a "Help Meet" can overwhelm even the mentally strong when used out of order. You, the woman, were created to HELP not "DO." This may be a tough pill to swallow but choking on the truth is better than living a lie. You were designed to help, assist, enhance, and add to but not DO. What do I mean? Whenever you attempt to "DO" something you end up taking on the responsibility of another by carrying it as your own, which can lead to stress, weariness, and frustration. When you assist or help with a challenge or task you give yourself permission to whoever is willing to affirm her and make her feel needed.

You have been tailored to succeed therefore success is inevitable if you are willing to take responsibility for your role as God takes responsibility for His. You do play a part. If you and I were playing a game of tennis and I served the ball in your direction, without any effort on your part to hit it back, it is safe to say that you will lose the game. You did not lose because it was God's desire but because you did not take responsibility of making an effort. Success is the fruit that comes from making an effort, even if it requires multiple tries.

YOU DO PLAY A PART

As a woman regardless of your status, married or single, there is no excuse for aborting the gifts and vision within you. Never lose who you are due to a relationship, circumstance, or limitation. Marriage is a beautiful union when both male and female are purpose driven in unity. He respects the level of strength and creativity that she possesses as she submissively recognizes his strength and vision as the man. Even as a married woman God will marry your vision into your husband's vision as you become one.

Single ladies are not void of purpose but are positioned for the ability to be intentional about cultivating their gifts until they are divinely connected to the man. There is a difference in being emotionally lonely and being alone. It is easy for a single woman to enter into the emotional handicap of loneliness because she has taking her eyes off her vision. As a "temporary" single woman, notice I said TEMPORARY, reject the emotion of feeling incomplete because you are single. As a single woman myself I have grown to understand through the word of God and have embraced that I am already complete because I am complete in Him who created me.

Complete in Him who created me sounds clique right; only to those looking outside of God to find success and completeness. The trappings of success will entrap you if you gain them outside of understanding the One who initially opened the door and gave you the wisdom to possess them. Your purpose is not tied up in what you have but who you are and your assignment for existing. Things and prestige are a bi-product of you taking responsibility and operating in your role.

If I were to ask you to tell me about yourself, who you are, it is safe to say that you would identify yourself by your marital status, the number of children you have had, job position, degrees earns, or businesses owned. Listen to the question, I was not asking you to articulate the area that you have helped in or as some may say, "what you do" but I was asking, "Who Are You?" Who you are is not tied up in what you do but rather in "Why" you were created and "Who" you are assigned to help. Do not lose who you are. Your success is wrapped up in who you are as a person not as a title: mother, wife, sister, aunt, teacher, graduate`, doctor, entrepreneur, inventor, etc.

The outer appearance seen by others may not reflect the inner potential that lies dormant within you but that does not negate that you were created to give birth to destiny. The birthing vessel known as the womb is not limited to just conceiving children. The birthing vessel also has the ability to birth visions and dreams; while assisting others in the birthing process.

THE BIRTHING OF A WOMAN

The pain that accompanies the process of going through labor is excruciating as she awaits the breaking of her water. The only thought running through her head at that particular moment is how unbearable the contractions are. "Why did I allow myself to go through this?" she asks herself quietly under her breath as her husband holds her hand. The purity of water that flows down her legs initiates the process and positions the birthing of something priceless, one of God's greatest creations…WOman. As she holds her newly born baby girl she forgets the agony of the birth and pressure from the labor pains the doctor had previously guided her through. The mother, the help meet proclaims out loudly the joy of being blessed with such a gift forgetting that she ever experienced birth pains. Pain can misdirect your sight from the beauty of the process that is vitally necessary.

Can you feel it? Your baby is moving. You may be experiencing temporary labor pains depending on how far along you are. As you read this book there is a baby developing within you: the baby of untapped potential, vision, creativity, and ideas. You do not have to be with child physically to be pregnant with purpose; every journey toward its manifestation brings with it labor pains in the form of obstacles, fears, and mistakes.

Who you are is not tied up in what you do but rather in "Why" you were created and "Who" you are assigned to help.

What does it mean to give birth? To give birth is the process of extracting or bringing forth something from seed form, be it a seed that come from a thought, human, or even a plant. Ideas are birth, vegetation and fruits are birth, and humans are birth because everything produces from a seed of its own kind. When society thinks of giving birth many often limit it to the birthing of a child when in essence it is much broader. You may use another word to describe its formation but everything that exists was birth from something.

Whereas the bible uses the word "Man" to identify male; this same terminology encompasses WOman as well:

> So God created man in His own image; in the image of God He created him; male and female He created THEM. Then God blessed THEM, and said to THEM, "Be fruitful and multiply; fill the earth and subdue it; have dominion…. (Genesis 1:27-28).

Before WOman was sculptured from man God released a blessing over both male and female which preceded fruitfulness and multiplication, fulfillment, the ability to conquer and live in dominion. The blessing did not stop at man, it overshadowed WOman as well. When God released "The Blessing" over man and WOman He released the anointing to operate at a level in the earth that mirrored His image. CATCH IT….God anointed WOman to mimic His image in the earth through giving birth and operating in a level of authority in the earth along with man.

When God released "The Blessing" over man and WOman He released the anointing to operate at a level in the earth that mirrored His image.

Prayer: Lord God I honor You and acknowledge my dependency on You. I accept the W.O.M.A.N. that You have created and tailored me to be and I will not limit You by limiting my gifts. I look to You Lord. I trust You to give me the grace and wisdom to birth forth the purpose that You have impregnated me with. Use me Lord to bring life to those who are hurting. Thank You Lord for blessing the works of my hands.

Do you have an understanding of who God is and the purpose of why you where created? Explain.

_____
_____
_____
_____
_____
_____

Let's identify your purpose: Is there a business developing within you or perhaps an intellectual property in the form of a product you plan to manufacture? Could it be that within you there is a desire for a higher education or could it be the desire of investing in real estate or commodities like oil, gas, and coins? Is there a book moving around inside you that you are laboring to write? Have you been fashioned to bring life into the broken soul of the hurting or is there a ministry within you? What is it that you are pregnant with?

_____
_____
_____

_____
_____
_____
_____
_____
_____

A Help Mate is one who is called to feel a need where there is a void. She is a servant leader. Who and where is your gift called to serve?

_____
_____
_____
_____
_____
_____
_____
_____

As a woman how do you see yourself? Presently, how do you see yourself? Do you see yourself as inferior or as an overcomer, bound by your past or free to walk toward your future, rejected or accepted? Do you see yourself as God sees you, beautifully and wonderfully made, anointed and appointed to be fruitful and multiply or as man sees you? How do you see yourself? The truth will set you free....

_____
_____

_____
_____
_____
_____
_____
_____
_____
_____

Although God will fulfill His part, you do play apart in the birthing process of your success. What does "Taking Responsibility" mean to you?

_____
_____
_____
_____
_____
_____
_____
_____

TWO

The Enemy to Your Success

> THE LAST THING THAT GOD CREATED IS THE FIRST THING THAT SATAN DECLARED WAR ON...THE WOMAN.
>
> ~Pastor Hart Ramsey

Have you ever wondered why you as a woman experience so many obstacles, pains, and challenges? Not negating that men will not experience hardship or pain but women arguably carry greater burdens than men. Who is she: the daughter, wife, lover, mother, employee, entrepreneur, house cleaner, cook, counselor, encourager, problem solver, prayer warrior simultaneously? From the beginning of time God established a very important fact, the woman and her enemy (satan) would have enmity or hostility towards one another. The enemy to your success is SATAN. He devises countless plans every moment of every day on how he can distract, deceive, destroy, overwhelm, manipulate, and even kill you. I am not saying that everything that happens to the woman is satan's responsibility because many challenges and pains that women experience are a result of poor decision making but many of them are attacks contrived by her enemy. The good news is once she begins to understand his strategies and learns how to use the power that is available to her she will be unstoppable. Satan is not after you he is after what lies within you…..The Word of God and Your Purpose.

You are the seed carrier, and within every seed lie something greater than itself. The seed within you that holds your purpose is similar to the apple seed; although tiny and seemingly insignificant it holds within it the ability to produce something much large than itself. The end result of the apple seed is a massive tree, which has the ability within to produce an orchard. Within you lay not only the ability to birth children but also ideas, visions, and dreams. It is vital that every hindrance to your success be exposed and terminated.

Satan is not after you he is after what lies within you…
The Word of God and Your Purpose.

This chapter will unveil several potential enemies to your success that can threaten to stop your forward movement. Later in chapter five we will shed light on the feelings of pain that can linger for years like an unwanted shadow of darkness over your life. Pain often comes from traumatic feelings of rejection, negative confessions (whether personally or from a loved one), abuse, and overwhelming obligations. This chapter is not designed to motivate but rather to bring awareness to women who have decided that average is no longer good enough. They are intentionally seeking an understanding of why they feel stuck. Just like battle, you must understand your enemy and his mode of operation for destroying you. Developing your knowledge gives you an advantage over your adversary. Understanding who fights your battle gives you an uncommon advantage, along with a posture of boldness and confidence; you are aware that this is an unfair fight because God set the rules.

God never said that you would not experience affliction, but He did say that He will make a way of escape; He will give you the strength to overcome. He said that in Christ you always triumph. He also said that His strength is made perfect in weakness. The question is, "Who are you going to believe?" It took years to embrace those statements of truth. There was a battle going on inside me from past hurts, rejections, and misguidance from people who led me blindly. Yes I had a level of success and yes I had money but I was still broken on the inside. External success does not eliminate internal pain. The treasure case to healing and wholeness was unlocked to me once

I accepted that I needed God's help and was opened to whomever He would use to give me wisdom.

If your enemy can keep you stressed, depressed, and living in anxiety he can succeed in causing you to miscarry the seed that holds your destiny. Stress will leave you feeling confused and under pressure. Depression will overshadow you with a heavy emotional sadness. Anxiety will paralyze you with an overwhelming feeling of fear. Stress, depression, and anxiety are three of many emotional handicaps that can lead to years of delayed goals, plans, and ultimately your creativity and visions. These emotional diseases can surface whenever you take on responsibilities that are not yours, imprison yourself in unhealthy relationships, and when you stop pursuing purpose to focus on life's problems.

External success does not eliminate internal pain.

You were created and tailored to multi-task without having to feel overwhelmed. Take a moment and read the characteristics, roles, and responsibility of the woman known to many as the "Proverbs 31 woman" found in Proverbs 31:10-31. She was not only a wife and mother, she was also a giver, entrepreneur, tenacious, investor, athletic, philanthropist, creator, manufacturer, distributor, woman of wisdom and excellence; she was a great steward to her family. She was and still today is known as the virtuous woman. I am sure that she had disappointments, challenges, and unexpected issues but in spite it all she was polarized to the world as the Proverbs 31 Woman of Virtue. You, like the woman of virtue, were created to systematize many tasks but not to carry them as a burden.

TAKING OWNERSHIP

Self-awareness is vital to overcoming the enemy or enemies to your success. If you never take the time to identify the what, why, and how certain emotions attached themselves to your life they will prevent you from moving forward and taking action. Being self-aware is to be cognizant or conscious of those (including yourself) who have inflicted pain against you personally, whether physically or mentally. Many are in disbelief when they hear that they could have possibly played a role in self-inflicting emotional stress upon themselves. Self-inflicted emotional stress comes in play whenever you give a person or habit who are detrimental to your personal growth permission to remain there.

There are hundreds and possibly thousands of words to describe the enemies to your success but I will address some of the most prevalent: identity crisis, unforgiveness, and the power of negative confessions. With these enemies come confusion, self-denial, bitterness, low self-esteem, pride, doubt, and stagnation.

WHO'S IDENTITY ARE YOU LIVING?

As a child I was called many names that shaped my thinking about myself for many years. Many people, adults and children, would say constantly to me, "You are such a tomboy. Girl you are skinny like olive oil. You talk so loud. Did you know that you ask too many questions?" Although later in life those names began to change to, "you are pretty and smart" it took me years to believe them. Because I was called a skinny tomboy that gave me a reason to wear oversized clothing to hide my legs, play in trees, and climb houses with the neighborhood boys. I was so bruised mentally by how skinny I was that it took me until the age of 23 before I would ever wear a skirt in public other than when I was a cheerleader in high school. I was naturally an inquisitive child so asking questions fed my desire to learn but being made to feel ignorant for doing so caused me to shy away from asking questions even in school. People are ignorantly unaware that the words they speak over others, including their children can affect their ability mentally and physically for years.

Who are you really? You may have college degrees and possibly beautiful children and may even be married but who are you really? Maybe you have overcome years of abuse even rejection but who are you really? Yes, you even had the motivation to turn the naysayer's words against them by succeeding at what they said you would fail at but who are you really? Huh, just maybe you motivated yourself to go back to school, start that business, launch your ministry but the question that I am proposing to you is WHO ARE YOU REALLY? Until you can truly answer this question you will live in a world formed by the words and opinions of your parents, childhood friends, mentors, and even spouse.

Whenever you are experiencing a disturbance to your peace of who you are, why you were born, or a void of fulfillment you could be experiencing a form of Identity Crisis. Identity is the condition of being oneself whereas crisis is defined as a condition of instability. Therefore Identity Crisis is the condition of instability in being oneself. External success does not equate to internal freedom. Internal peace with oneself, regardless of life's trials, releases a freedom to live in a noisy world with invisible earplugs on. It is possible to live above your situation with emotional freedom in the midst of turmoil.

External success does not equate to internal freedom.

As you read the words on the pages of this book you may have it all together, life may be absolutely wonderful for you or maybe you are like so many women who are tired of living a lie based on others standards. Maybe you like wearing bright colors like yellow but you only wear blues and grays because that is what you have been taught to do. Maybe you desire to go back to school or start that business that you have always wanted to start but people say that you are too old. Whatever it is until you follow YOUR HEART you will give yourself permission to remain a victim versus a victor who overcame. Make the decision; give yourself permission to be authentic. God's desire is for you to be free internally and externally; authenticity brings with it FREEDOM.

FORGIVENESS LEADS TO HEALING

Ask yourself, "Is there anyone that I am harboring unforgiveness toward, including myself?" Asking yourself this question will unlock doors that have been closed for years so brace yourself.

Unforgiveness is like a deadly disease, it has the ability to start small then spread throughout your life destroying your peace, joy, happiness, and ultimately your purpose. I have heard women say that they could never forgive a person who took the life of their child. I have also heard women say that they would never forgive a man who have been unfaithful to them. Maybe you do not harbor hate or unforgiveness toward another but rather toward yourself. Constantly allowing yourself to feel like a failure in any area of life, whether as an entrepreneur, minister, friend, parent, spouse, or personally, is unforgiveness directed toward self. Regardless of what it is and how painful it may have been there is nothing unforgiveable, even your own personal mistakes. Nothing is unforgiveable. You may disagree but God does not.

I am so grateful to God for His grace because it is God's grace that gives us the ability and strength to forgive those who have inflicted pain toward us even when we think that we emotionally cannot. I am not saying that you will not feel hurt, betrayed, disappointed but I am saying that if you look to God to help you to forgive He will. If you harden your heart and are adamant about not forgiving you have chosen to walk in pride and the bible reminds us that pride comes before a fall. You are love because God is love, and you are made in His image, therefore you have it embedded within your DNA to love and to forgive, even yourself. Unforgiveness gives your enemy power OVER you because whenever you choose to remain bitter you decide to partner with the one who desires to kill you (satan). When you make the conscious decision to forgive, the enemy plans for your life will begin to dissipate.

Forgiveness releases the power of imprisonment from your life.

Forgiveness releases the power of imprisonment from your life. Unforgiveness is a form of imprisonment to your soul. If you have unforgiveness in your heart my prayer for you is that you release it. Ask God for the grace to forgive yourself and those who wronged you in any way. Forgiveness will start the healing process in your life and unclog the blessings that you have held up because of unforgiveness.

And whenever you stand praying, if you have anything against anyone, forgive him that your Father in heaven may also forgive you your trespasses. But if you do not forgive, neither will your Father in heaven forgive your trespasses (Mark 11:25-26).

YOUR WORDS HAVE LIFE

While growing up my mother was on drugs, and because of that my siblings and I were the community joke; that led to me constantly fighting to defend my family from embarrassment. Many would say that I had no positive role model but I would object to their opinion. While my mom was bound by the addiction of drugs she still tried to provide for her four children and discipline us when needed. My birthday is on July fourth, although it is popularly known as the fourth of July. Every year my beautiful mother, who is now deceased, would bake many pies and cakes, along with a host of food, invite friends over and say to me, "baby you see everybody around the world is celebrating your birthday." Those were words of life that I say even to this day although I know otherwise. My mother was celebrating me in her own special way with her own unique words of life.

I often refer to the bible when I want to remind myself of truth versus facts. The bible speaks truth whereas what you are experiencing presently is a fact. As women of purpose we must grow the habit of speaking only words of truth over our lives, words that we desire to see come to reality, versus words of fact or death. Many women make the error of speaking words out of their mouth that they do not desire to see come to pass. For example: if you are experiencing financial lack, and a person ask you how are you doing, and you reply, "I am not doing well, I cannot pay my bills. I am always broke." you will remain there. Whatever you focus on will be your end result. We are reminded to call those things that be not as though they were, yet many are calling those things that should not be as they are. Purpose, visions, and ideas lack the wisdom, resources, and connections it needs to reach its full potential not because they were not available but because negative words of belief prevented them from manifesting.

Whatever you focus on will be your end result.

Words have life and what we constantly release into the atmosphere by faith will come eventually to pass whether positive or negative. Proverbs 18:20 reminds us that "Death and life is in the power of the tongue and those who love it will eat its fruit." in other words whatever you speak will produce fruit that you will eat. It is possible to give birth to something negative if you believe it to be so. Whatever is spoken by faith over time will remain in your life or eventually come to pass. If you constantly tell yourself that you are broke, you are too old to go to school, or you do not have what it take to accomplish your dreams your life will began to mimic your words. Mind renewal is required to speak consistent words of life over your situation. Practice replacing every negative word of death or fact, even when speaking about others, with words of truth and life.

ENEMIES TO YOUR SUCCESS

This is not an exhaustive list of enemies that can stagnate or abort your success but many women have or are currently experiencing:

- *Depression
- *Bitterness
- *Stress
- *Low Self-Esteem
- *Lack of Prayer
- *Feelings of Unworthiness
- *Poor Self-Image
- *Soul Ties
- *Negative Association
- *Negative Words
- *Murmuring/Complaining
- *Addiction of Any Kind
- *Feeling Rejected
- *Fear
- *Gossip
- *Self Pity
- *Excuses
- *People Pleaser
- *Poor Stewardship
- *Judgmental Attitude
- *Anxiety
- *Unforgiveness
- *Lack of Rest
- *Worry
- *Self Dependency
- *Confusion
- *Self Sabotage
- *Apathy
- *Busyness
- *Poor Eating Habits
- *Abuse
- *Unbelief
- *Pride
- *Impatience
- *Laziness
- *Procrastination
- *Lack of Planning
- *Lack of Action
- *Insecurity
- *Passivity

*Bad Decision Making   *Hate

    Although this is not an exhaustive list of enemies hopefully you will be cognizant of what to look for so whenever one of them surface you can return it back to the sender, your #1 enemy satan. I have personally experienced an attack by most if not all of the enemies aforementioned. I can speak only for myself; the only weapon that I have found that has brought me to a place of victory was the word of God and positive confessions of faith consistently while often shedding many tears. It was not easy but I just refused to be overcome with grief and feelings of defeat.

    I learned who I was and who I am by learning who Christ is and the authority that God has given me through Him. The benefit of internalizing scriptures from God's word is that when the enemy would surface I would begin instantly declaring the word out of my mouth until I began to enter a place of rest. Entering this place of rest is a decision, a choice that you will not succumb or submit to the enemy's tactics any longer. God's rest is available to you, enter it.

> **I learned who I was by learning who Christ is and the authority that God has given me through *Him*.**

Prayer: Lord forgive me for carrying unforgiveness in my heart and for doubting Your ability to free me from my current situations. God, by Your Spirit, remind me whenever I speak words contrary to Your Word, the truth. Help me to know who I am and Your purpose for my life so that I may live in my true identity. Thank You Lord for the grace to forgive and live. Amen!

Self-Awareness is vital to you overcoming the enemies to your success. List the enemies that have held you in a state of paralysis, preventing you from moving forward. Be honest with yourself.

_____
_____
_____
_____
_____
_____
_____
_____

God said that His strength is made perfect in your weakness; what does this statement mean to you?

_____
_____
_____
_____
_____
_____
_____
_____

Why is "Self-Awareness" important?

_____
_____
_____
_____
_____
_____

Are you speaking any negative words over yourself or anyone else, if so what are they? Now write down the positive word that you will replace the negative word with, even in a challenge.

_____
_____
_____
_____
_____
_____
_____
_____
_____

Whose identity are you living; is it the identity that your family and friends conditioned your mind to or is it the identity God tailored you to be? Be honest with yourself.

_____
_____
_____
_____
_____
_____
_____
_____

What would stop you from doing what you really felt passionate about and led to do?

_____
_____
_____
_____
_____

Believe God to the End!

THREE

Where Is Your Trust?

IN GOD I HAVE PUT MY TRUST; I WILL NOT BE AFRAID.
WHAT CAN MAN DO TO ME?
~Psalm 56:11

Sometimes it is the painful moments that unlock the door to your power. Have you ever asked this question "Why Me?" whenever a painful challenge introduces itself into your life often unexpectedly? This is a question that many ask whenever they focus more on the pain that comes as a result of the situation versus the lesson or power that could be gained from it. Pain is an evitable feeling that we will all experience in our lives whether physical or emotional. Pain is defined as a physical, mental, or emotional suffering or distress. Let's put emphasis on the word "Suffering". Suffering is a **prolonged** state of being and until we understand that prolonged suffering comes from focusing on the wrong thing continual distress will remain.

I recently had the opportunity of experiencing a painful moment "briefly" in my life. Let's look at two words: opportunity and briefly. I chose to highlight the word "briefly" because I have grown to understand that I have been given the power of choice. I can either choose to remain in a state of pain, which will translate into suffering, or I can choose to release it by growing from of it. Opportunity is defined as a chance for advancement. Every challenging circumstance is an **opportunity** for your advancement spiritually and personally. Do you believe that? If not, the pain could translate into prolonged suffering.

> Every challenging circumstance is an opportunity for your advancement spiritually and personally.

By no means am I negating the fact that you will not feel pain, hurt, disappointment, or feel like giving up after you have chosen to grow through it. What I am relaying is this, because you have chosen not to partner with the pain or situation the healing process can begin.

A lesson learned releases another level of power and potential. Yes, pain may have **visited** my life but I am elated to share with you that I learned a valuable lesson; I located myself and took advantage of the opportunity presented before me. The lesson learned started my journey on the road of learning the power "IN" trusting God versus trusting in me, my circumstances, or even man (which includes woman). This has been one of the greatest lessons of my life, and I share this revelation every opportunity that I get. We are called to honor and respect man but not to put our trust IN them or things. We are commanded to put our trust IN the living God.

> A lesson learned releases another level of power and potential.

THE DANGER "IN" TRUSTING MAN

We all have made the error of putting our trust IN people and things whether consciously or unconsciously only to end up disappointed and hurt. What is TRUST? To trust is to rely on or put confidence in the ability, strength, surety, or integrity of a person or thing.

We are reminded in Proverbs 3:5 to trust IN the Lord with all our hearts and lean not on our own understanding. Emphasis placed on the word "IN" because whenever you trust IN a person or thing you access all that it is. For example: the word of God instructs us to trust IN the Lord because He understands that whoever trust IN Him will access ALL that He is. We will access His peace, joy, freedom, anointing, healing, grace, love, protection, power, wisdom, strategies, favor, presence, righteousness, revelation, signs and wonders, provision, open doors, restoration, etc. The same is true for man, whenever you put your trust IN man you access ALL that he is. Jeremiah 17:9 said it best, "The heart is deceitful above all things and desperately wicked; who can know it?" therefore; when you put your trust IN man you access deceit, wickedness, inconsistency, instability, and confusion. I encourage you to give attention to the danger in putting your trust and focus IN the wrong places.

> Thus says the Lord: Cursed is the man who trusts in man and makes flesh his strength, whose heart departs from the Lord. For he shall be like a shrub in the desert, and shall not see when good comes, but shall inhabit the parched places in the wilderness, in a salt land which is not inhabited (Jeremiah 17:5, 6).

This passage begins by quoting what our Lord said, "cursed is the man who trusts IN man". As born again believers we know that Jesus' blood freed us from the curse of the enemy, so it is our own will and choices that can open us up to a world of destruction and distress not because God desires that for us but because of our own personal choice to operate outside of His will and word. The verse goes on to reveal that when your focus is on man, which includes yourself, rather than God your heart has departed from Him which leads to a lower level of living, blindness to the goodness of God, and inhabiting dry places.

Whenever you trust IN God you access ALL that He is.

Have you ever felt stagnated, confused, or like God is blessing everyone excluding you. Maybe your focus or trust is off. Maybe you are giving more attention to people and things versus the One who empowers you to take possession, which is the Almighty God.

How do you seek advice from a mentor, coach, Pastor, friend, or love one without feeling like you are putting your trust IN them? How do you make a personal decision without feeling like you're trusting IN your own efforts or understanding? Ask yourself these questions before making a decision: Is this God's will for my life? Did God instruct me to do this? Do I have a peace in my spirit regarding this decision? Does this decision line up with God's word? Have I thought through it to envision what the end result could be? The only way to truly answer these questions is to seek God first for the answer and trust that He will reveal the truth to you. There is nothing detrimental in seeking sound counsel if you do it in the proper order but never put man before God because that will be a detrimental decision.

TRUST "IN" THE LORD

To trust IN God is to access all that He is. What an amazing truth in knowing that it is your trust, faith, and obedience that opens you up to uncommon results not unbelief. Unbelief leads to delay of God's promises manifesting in your life, along with a life of confusion and stagnation. Like so many, I to viewed unbelief as a lack of faith until I heard a profound teaching on faith by my Pastor, Dr. Michael D. Moore; he said:

> Unbelief is not non-belief because we are always believing, unbelief is misdirected belief. Some Christians have great faith in the wrong things. The object of our faith is where we are focusing our trust because our faith is always working.

It is possible to trust IN man more than you trust IN God. It is possible to trust IN things more than your trust IN God. It is possible to trust IN your own ability more than you trust IN God. Your faith can be directed toward something outside of God. But when you trust in God ALL things are made possible for you.

Let's take a journey through Proverbs 3:5, 6 because when you go from quoting this passage of scripture to living it that is the moment when your life will transform forever. The passage begins with eight powerful words, "Trust IN the Lord with all your heart"; we have already established the truth that trusting IN God gives you access to all that He is. Verse 5 continues by instructing you to, "Lean not ON your own understanding"; whenever you lean "on" something you are trusting that it will support you. Therefore, leaning on your own understanding will lead you into trusting in your own ability versus Gods. Proverbs 6 also gives instructions by stating "In all your ways acknowledge Him"; whenever you acknowledge God despite your feelings or desires you surrender your will to His. Verse 6 concludes with a promise, "And He shall direct your paths." submission to God's will makes you sensitive to hearing His voice and instructions.

    Earlier in the chapter I highlighted Jeremiah 17:5, 6 where it stated that cursed is the man who trusts in man but the great news is in the latter verses 7 and 8 it reminds the believer of additional blessings connected to putting their faith and trust in the Lord God.

> Blessed is the man who trusts in the Lord, and whose hope is the Lord. For he shall be like a tree planted by the waters, which spreads out its root by the river, and will not fear when heat comes; but its leaf will be green, and will not be anxious in the

year of drought, nor will cease from yielding fruit (Jeremiah 17:7, 8).

What amazing promises! Who would not want to access that level of peace, protection, security, and fruitfulness? This promise is a reminder that all who trust IN the Lord will be planted by the waters, which represents the Word; there is life in the Word of God. Not only will you be planted but you will expand and not be shaken when challenges come because your trust is not in the challenge but IN the Lord. The promise concludes by reminding those who put their trust IN God that in spite of obstacles they will continue to be fruitful and progress.

We are all giving a measure of faith but it is up to each individual person to build their faith muscle by studying faith in order to gain an in-depth understanding of how it works and how to work it. Faith, the audacity to trust God and His word, will provoke the miraculous in your life.

GIVE YOURSELF A CHANCE

Have you every just sat and thought to yourself the impact that you could really make in this world and in the lives of others if you just gave yourself a chance to succeed? On July 6th I posted a message on facebook that I would like to share with you that reads:

Ask yourself this question: What could I really do if I gave myself a REAL chance to succeed? I mean REMOVING the opinions of what people may think, what people may say, removing every limiting thought of how I do not qualify. What gifts would I expose to this world if I just gave myself the opportunity that I so often give others? Huh, what if I removed the thought of who is not supporting me, who have chosen to walk away? What would happen if I TOTALLY trusted God to open doors, connect me to new people, and provide the wisdom, favor, and provision I need to flourish? What untapped potential would I really expose to myself and this world? Food for thought.

We give people, circumstances, and the devil to much of our power.

It might sound repetitive but it is worth repeating: winning is intentional, living a life of peace is a choice, and succeeding is optional. We give people, circumstances, and the devil to much of our power. Quitting, complaining, making excuses not to move forward, etc. is a form of giving your power away to the person you are complaining about or the obstacle that you are focusing on. Give yourself the opportunity to succeed because God has. He desires for you to experience Him in an amazing and supernatural way, not just naturally but spiritually. The power that comes from "trusting" IN the Lord…meditate on it, study it, and make it a lifestyle; your life will never be the same if you do. Faith unlocks the door to the impossible.

> Give yourself the opportunity to succeed because God has.

Prayer: Lord, forgive me if I have trusted more in man than I have in You; forgive me if I have trusted more in my own strength than I have in You. I love You Father and it is my heart's desire to solely trust in You. Teach me Your ways Lord. Feel me with the knowledge of Your will for my life. I choose to trust in You only. Thank You for Your faithfulness towards me. Amen!

Proverbs 3:5, 6 and Jeremiah 17:5-9 highlights the importance of trusting in God versus man. Why is it important to put your trust solely in God?

_____
_____
_____
_____
_____
_____
_____
_____

What is the downside to putting your trust in man, which includes your own strength?

_____
_____
_____
_____
_____
_____
_____
_____

What does the words "TRUST IN" means to you?

_____
_____
_____
_____
_____
_____

_____

_____

_____

Have you every just sat and thought to yourself the impact that you could make in this world and in the lives of others if you just gave yourself a chance to succeed? Explain.

_____

_____

_____

_____

_____

_____

_____

Have you really put your trust "IN" God? If not, are you willing to learn and understand what it means to trust "IN" Him versus man? What steps are you willing to take to start the learning process?

_____

_____

_____

_____

_____

_____

_____

FOUR

Positioned for Purpose
Why Not You?

UNTIL YOU ACCEPT YOURSELF, NO OTHER ACCEPTANCE WILL MATTER

Arion is her name; a woman of many gifts and talents. She is known for her creative touch, electric voice, and her ability to serve leaders, which became her way of life. The challenge that she battled with was her inability to decipher between serving leaders and operating in her gift of leading. She felt disqualified to be out front because her only place of familiarity was behind the scene. For years countless people would encourage her to use her gift of motivating because through speaking she had the unique ability to inspire all who encountered her. Sadly enough Arion was unwilling to accept her own gifts although others had, and because of self denial she delayed her potential for many years. Until you accept yourself, no other acceptance will matter.

True acceptance of oneself can seem so hard when life has consumed you with obligations, responsibilities, and expectations. "I do accept myself!" you may boldly proclaim but if so why do you feel a sense of internal emptiness, which has led to external stagnation? Acceptance of oneself is simply approval of who you are your uniqueness, talents, gifts, and purpose. Have you approved of your own dreams and visions or are you awaiting the validation of someone else? Waiting on the validation of another will leave you WAITING. As a woman of purpose do not make the error of seeking validation of man versus wise counsel from man. Before God created you in your mother's womb He validated you as a woman of potential and purpose. God uses man, which includes woman, to give wise counsel when needed. We are reminded that in a multitude of counsel, not validation, there is safety.

Be cautious when seeking counsel or advice from others; make sure whomever you choose to counsel with has a pure heart and motive toward you. Jealousy and covetousness can lead to judgmental and destructive advice because you chose to divulge your vision to someone whose motive and heart was not toward you. Protecting your vision will keep you in a position of purpose. Negativity has a way of distorting your view and moving you off the path of purpose. Protect your vision at all cost.

Acceptance of oneself is simply approval of who you are: your uniqueness, talents, gifts, and purpose.

Positioned for a purpose; every challenge, obstacle, trial, and test positioned you for this very moment. Your critics may have bruised you, bent, broke, talked about, or polished you, but they did not kill you. Thank God for every opportunity you were given to grow into the woman that you are today.

YOU WERE BORN FOR THIS

Have you ever asked yourself or maybe even God the question, "If this is what I am born to do then why am I experiencing so much emotional pain and so many natural challenges?" The next time that question attempts to develop in your mind declare aloud before you ask it, "I WAS BORN FOR THIS!!!" Always remember this one truth stated by Pastor Michael D. Moore, "God is not limited to natural and physical laws or human limitations and your faith trumps (supersedes) natural and physical laws and human limitations." Internalizing the Word of God will renew your mind, which will set the course of your life. Whatever God has assigned you to do, regardless of limitations, He has made possible if you would only believe.

> But Jesus looked at them and said, "With men *it is* impossible, but not with God; for with God all things are possible." (Mark 10:27)

Internalizing the Word of God will renew your mind, which will set the course of your life.

Everything that you need to move forward into destiny has already been made available for you. Your physical eyes will not see what your spiritual eyes of faith will. God will never assign you a vision without releasing provision. Provision is connected to your faith and obedience to God; either you trust Him or you don't. You were born to rule and reign in the earth but if you do not believe this truth it will profit you nothing. It is of high importance that you believe in two areas, one being God's capability, two your worthiness to be used in spite of any limitations. If you believe in one and not the other delay of your future is inevitable.

Are you a dreamer in pursuit of purpose? Dream chasers often get discouraged because they chase the vision versus the one who gives wisdom to manifest the vision into their reality. Whenever you chase or run after a goal or dream you will find yourself depending on your own efforts and leaning toward your own wisdom. Your focus is off. Running will leave you tired and restless because you are running after something that does not exist….things from God. Once I grew to understand this one truth my life entered into a place of peace and rest. God does not give things; He gives wisdom, ability, strategies, favor, ideas, connections, and open doors to get things but He does not give you things. He can touch someone's heart to give you things but He has never giving things but rather wisdom and guidance to get or create things.

God does not make mistakes, He makes potential.

Re-calibrate your focus. As a woman in pursuit of purpose, look to the one who gives vision. Ask for wisdom to make wise decisions, strategies to maximize your time and develop the vision, favor to access things that money cannot buy, and relationships that will use their influence and resources to help you. Remember, God Almighty can use whomever He chooses to bless you. He can open any door of favor He chooses to display your gifts, but you must accept who you are and understand that God does not make mistakes, He makes potential. Potential is untapped ability that develops overtime the more it is utilized. Potential lies within you ready to be challenged. Make the decision to place a demand on your potential by placing a demand on yourself to go forward. You have been positioned on purpose for a purpose, and you were born for this.

YOU ARE NOT GOOD ENOUGH?

"SAYS WHO?!" should be your reply in the form of a question whenever you hear the words that you are not good enough, smart enough, talented enough, have enough. Well, enough is enough. There are over six billion people on planet earth and there is no one, male nor female, whose finger print matches yours. Statements attempting to evaluate your self-worth based on your qualifications as a women are statements of ignorance. People speak out of ignorance not because they do not care but because of a lack of knowledge. Ignorance simply means a lack of knowledge. The person addressing you apparently have not become knowledgeable about who you were before you were ever born. The creation of the woman speaks for itself – purpose is a part of her DNA.

You are not good enough because you were designed to be greater *than good.*

I am guilty of speaking erroneously over personal areas of my life due to a lack of understanding of who I was and the importance of my scripted role on this stage called life. As mentioned earlier, self-awareness is vital to releasing unhindered potential. If you currently view yourself as being disqualified as Arion viewed herself, mind renewal is required. It is not your fought that you were rejected, abused, belittled, and made to feel inferior, but it will be your fought if you allow yourself to be defined by those lies. You are not good enough because you were designed to be greater than good. You were great enough then, and you are great enough now. Do not base your worth on outer accomplishments, money, or prestige. Base your worth on whose identity you were created in and in doing so material things and prestige will never be able to define your worth even when you obtain them.

IF NOT YOU, THEN WHO?

Positioning is about alignment. Alignment is to adjust something or someone properly. You can scream aloud, "I am woman and I am born for this!" and feel no motivation to move forward in life. I repeat....positioning is about alignment, proper adjustment. Positioning is about re-aligning your old way of thinking and replacing it with a new mindset. If there is no adjustment made in how you view yourself and your assignment words alone will be like an empty balloon with no air - flat. Spoken words not preceded by action are void of life, resulting in no results. A woman who demonstrates her enthusiasm and faith through actions versus mere words is a woman of fruitfulness and productivity. Faith is an action word, mere words alone does not equate to faith. James validated this point by recording in the Word of God:

> But someone will say, "You have faith, and I have works." Show me

your faith without your works, and I will show you my faith by my works (James 2:18).

Never allow yourself to be deceived in believing that faith is "waiting", NO, faith is "working". Working can mean resting in peace versus worrying in the midst of a life challenge or obeying the instructions of God in spite of natural limitations. If God instructed you to start a business or ministry with limited resources would you lean to your own understanding or would you trust in Him to provide as you step out in action by faith?

In chapter one I shared why the creation of woman was of great importance and why she was tailored for a purpose on purpose. Do you know what your purpose is? Do you have any idea why you exist at this very moment? Why did you survive the heartbreaking pains of life when there are those who did not? Why are you pursuing purpose, is it because you now understand that you are a woman of purpose whose strength lies not in your own ability but in Gods? Do you know your purpose but fear has paralyzed you? If you will not, who will? I asked you several thought provoking questions with the purpose of getting you to recognize the urgency in why you must not quit on your passion, your purpose. Your life is much larger than you. As a woman I understand the demands of life be it marriage, children, work, school, health challenges, business, etc., but there is more, and you have been equipped to handle it.

A woman who demonstrates her enthusiasm through actions versus mere words is a woman of fruitfulness and productivity.

Every woman on planet earth has been assigned to someone for the purpose of empowering them in some capacity. You are not an island, alone and detached from civilization. You are a seed of life, and there are people assigned to you that need to grow beyond their place of only physically existing. Your gift is connected to their survival as a person because it is through your gifts of inspiration, wisdom, and creativity that impartation of greatness will produce in their lives. If you do not answer the call, who will? Some women make the error of assuming that a personal no to themselves will stop there. Whenever you allow fear, procrastination, laziness, or feelings of low self-worth to hinder your performance you stifle your growth and the growth of all who are assigned to you. There are people that you have yet to meet that will cross your path after you say yes to your God designed assignment. Regardless, your gift is for the purpose of serving and helping others in need.

GIVE IT ALL YOU GOT

When our back is up against the wall tragedy has a way of pushing us as women into giving it all we got. I am encouraging you not to wait until a tragedy hits, give it all you got right now. That may mean detaching from poisonous relationships who are judgmental, negative, and de-edifying. That may mean disconnecting from destructive habits of laziness, procrastination, and busyness; because busyness does not equate to productivity. That may also mean enhancing your life by learning and doing new activities that will put you in diverse environments that add value: reading development books, going to networking events, traveling more, or acquiring a mentor. Success does not just happen, it must be intentional.

As a widow I personally know firsthand what it means to give it all you got. As a homemaker, mother, and college student my focus was not on paying bills because my husband took on that responsibility, but shortly after he passed unexpectedly that responsibility quickly transferred to me. As a single mother with no income, newly started home-base business, and insurance money tied up legally I had to make a decision and make it quick. I made the decision to build my business versus getting a job because I had no real work experience. I decided to give it all I had and trust God for the outcome. Fast forward, I became extremely successful at that business and was able to maintain financially before the insurance money was paid.

Success does not just happen, it must be intentional.

Life consist of a series of decisions, either you can decide to run toward the fire or away from it. Like a firefighter, the only way to take control of the flames is to run toward it not from it. Yes, you may not have the college degrees, know the right people, have the resources, or even have the wisdom to move forward but you do have the gift, potential, and capacity to give it all you got. Believe this truth: faith will release the favor, wisdom, relationships, and resources you need to operate within the confines of your capacity. Fear is not as powerful as you give it permission to be. You are one decision away from an amazing fulfilling life of peace and happiness. Give it all you got rest patiently and trust God for the outcome. God will bless the works of your hands.

Fear is not as powerful as you give it permission to be.

Prayer: Lord I am grateful to be chosen by You. Thank You for reminding me that I am great enough. Thank You for accepting me as I am. Show me where my life is out of alignment then give me the wisdom required to reposition myself for Your purpose. I say yes to Your assignment for my life Lord. I will give it all I got by faith, trusting You for the outcome. I will not allow fear to reign over my life anymore. Thank You Lord for giving me authority over fear. Amen!

Have you accepted your unique gifts? Have you accepted your unique self?

_____
_____
_____
_____
_____

WHY NOT YOU? Identify five reasons why you are worthy?

_____
_____
_____
_____
_____
_____
_____

Are you a dreamer in pursuit of purpose? What are you presently pursuing?

_____
_____
_____
_____
_____

Do you know what your purpose is?

_____
_____
_____
_____
_____
_____

Goal setting is very important to identifying where you are going and a plan of action is the road map to getting you there. Always be open to God altering your plan. Write down five goals that you will accomplish in the next 12 months. Discipline yourself to write them daily. Writing your goals daily will remind you of where you are going and eliminate any discouragement that may surface later.

_____
_____
_____
_____
_____
_____
_____
_____
_____

Are you speaking positive words of life over yourself, assignment, family, and life? If not why?

_____
_____
_____
_____
_____
_____
_____

FIVE

Pain will Paralyze Your Power

**PAIN WILL ONLY REMAIN
WHERE IT HAS PERMISSION TO RESIDE**

"Beloved, do not be amazed *and* bewildered at the fiery ordeal which is taking place to test your quality, as though something strange (unusual and alien to you and your position) were befalling you" 1 Peter 4:12 (AMP). Apostle Peter reminded us that trials are inevitable and not to think it strange but rather to rejoice in the midst of the test regardless of how painful it may seem. Life challenges will test the quality of who you are and will reveal where your faith lies. You were created to push through the pains which are meant to paralyze you.

Pain is a real emotion, which we all have experienced; dictionary.com defines it as a mental or emotional suffering or torment. Carrying pain can lead to mental and emotional suffering that often spills over into other areas of our lives: family, work, ministry, business, and friendships. I was recently at Wal-mart and while I was being served by the cashier I noticed on her countenance she was emotionally depressed. I asked, "How are you?' she replied, 'There is something wrong, there is something wrong with me." Because I understood the power of prayer and choice I asked her, "Do you believe that prayer can bring you to a place of peace?' she answered, 'yes." After she said yes I prayed a prayer of comfort over her and reminded her that regardless of what her problem was there is nothing that God cannot handle, choose to remain in peace by praying your way through the challenge. After conversing with her she thanked me and continued working. Without her saying a word I could feel the emotional suffering she was experiencing because it played out through the customer service she provided.

What is it, if any that ails you? Maybe you are a woman in pursuit of purpose who has overcome obstacles that once held you bound. I am in awe of God's faithfulness toward you and I am enthusiastically excited that you played a part in winning your peace back. If you are like so many women who feel stuck, overwhelmed, at times confused, and in emotional bondage what is it that ails you, which unlocked the door to pain? You may disagree, but LIVING WITH pain is a personal choice. Notice I did not say being in pain or experiencing pain, I said LIVING WITH it. To LIVE WITH something or someone, permission had to be given either on your part or theirs. There is a difference between pain visiting and pain abiding or living in your life. You may not be the one who caused the pain, but you are responsible for how long it resides with you. We can agree to disagree but give me the honor of continuing on by reading.

    When my mother, whom I loved beyond words, died unexpectedly in her sleep at the young age of 51 it literally took my breath away. The pain was unbearable. I cried the night of the incident so profusely it lead to me having an excruciating migraine headache for three days consecutively. Although, my mother birth four children I was the child who typically handled all of her affairs and business. I was responsible for planning the funeral, comforting my siblings, moving her things from her apartment, and raising money to bury her. It overwhelmed me because I believed that I had to perform these obligations while keeping a peaceful countenance; trying to hold my emotions in almost led to me having a nervous breakdown.

    I remember sitting in the parking lot of Books of Million crying because I felt lost and overwhelmed. I called my Pastor who began to minister to me; he shed light on why I was feeling so overwhelmed and consumed by my mother's death. As I began to receive the word that was spoken to me and embraced the peace that was available to me I instantly felt better. As the days passed I felt pain while mourning the loss of my dear mother but I decided that in the midst of it all I must continue to live my life in spite of the tears and hurt I felt, which I did. There is no greater loss than losing someone you love whether through death or divorce. Other losses can open the door to pain whether it be through the loss of a career, business, friendship, or a sentimental possession like a home. The pain will get lighter as you intentionally take the steps toward healing through reading the word of God, prayer, meditation, and counseling if necessary. The ultimate choice is up to YOU.

PUSH PAST THE PAIN

"I cannot push, the pain is unbearable!" this statement is only true when your focus is on the pain versus the promise to finish what you started. Think about it, whenever you make up in your mind that you will complete a goal or be intentional about fulfilling your purpose all hell breaks loose. One thing that is inevitable, life will happen to us all regardless of color, ethnicity, religion, or gender; you must decide up-front that you will not be stopped. Slowing down may be an option depending upon what you are faced with but stopping all together can result in the death of your vision. Like a mother giving birth, the pain can be unbearable but to release the gift within she must push and push and push until she finishes what she started or else she will risk the child's life. Her focus is not necessarily on the pain but on releasing what is causing the pain, because the final release will lead to relief.

> It is impossible to move forward when your mind only see the words "I Can't."

If your decision to put your goals and plans off until life gets better is your reason for pausing your plans, then you are giving yourself another reason to remain in a paralyzed state. Paralysis starts in the mind first, before it ever shows in your actions or decision making. Living in a paralyze state of mind is the inability to act. What you meditate on you eventually will do. If you allow the thought of "I cannot because it is unbearable" to replay itself over and over in your mind without taking authority over it by meditating on something positive your actions will result in inaction. It is impossible to move forward when your mind only see the words "I Can't."

Push past excuse making. Justifying your actions or lack thereof is a conservative word for excuse making. People who make excuses remain in the same state that they were in when they stopped pursuing their purpose. Excuses will result in paralysis. If you are experiencing stagnation due to a decision that delayed your goals then take ownership of your error without carrying guilt. Make the decision that you will not allow anything or anyone else to stop you from moving forward. Remember it is okay to slow down; slowing down may mean delegating someone to handle your business project or plans while you take care of unexpected issues. You may not be working directly with your plans but someone is working on your behalf. The worse thing that you can do when experiencing pain, hardship, or loss is to withdraw from the world to a secluded place alone for a period of time. A moment of withdrawal to reflect is one thing but seclusion is another. It is through the word, prayer, encouragement, positive affirmation, and inspiration that healing takes place. God uses people to inspire us just as He has utilized your gift of encouragement to inspire others. You are a woman of strength who was born to turn pain into power.

> *You are a woman of strength who was born to turn pain into power.*

PEOPLE ARE WAITING ON YOU

When I discovered that my assignment on earth was not totally about me but the people who I was called to serve, inspire, and mentor it increased my passion to overcome fear and excuses. Fear, excuses, impatience, and procrastination have stolen years of precious time from me only because I gave them permission to reside where I live. It is my goal to be as transparent as I can through the pages of this book. I am a woman of strength who has overcome many obstacles not because I am so special but because I sought God for the strength to overcome everything that was attempting to overcome me.

Fear and excuses will hinder your forward movement, impatience causes you to devalue the law of process -missing the opportunity to grow, and procrastination robs you of time, resources, and opportunities. Although, I have lost years, I have gained time back through the Law of Forward Movement. The Law of Forward Movement is the process of moving intentionally toward a targeted goal for the purpose of fulfilling it. God is the God of restoration, and He can restore the years that you lost as you walk forward by faith. Faith is powerful because it overshadows what you see presently with what you see to come.

Hold on to your visions, dreams, goals, and plans; hold on to your purpose. There are people awaiting your arrival. Whenever you say NO to your purpose you show a sign of weakness purposely. Whenever you say no to your purpose you say no not only to yourself but also God and all connected to your destiny. Your yes will bring healing to many because every female alive is connected to helping someone meet their purpose in this life. There are people in your family, job, business, and community that will listen to you before they listen to anyone else, but they are deterred by inconsistency, fear, and excuses. It is vital that you operate in the manner that you were created, as a woman of strength and purpose, designed as a help meet to help meet a need where there is a void.

AIN'T NO STOPPING US NOW

There is a popular song by McFadden and Whitehead that can be looked upon as an anthem of motivation as you take steps toward progress, and the chorus rings out, "Ain't no stopping us now, we are on the move." As you snap your fingers, with a smile on your face singing aloud you are reminding yourself that I have made a personal decision to move toward purpose because pain may visit, but it cannot set up residence here.

No one on earth has the power to stop you but you.

No one on earth has the power to stop you but you. You can be your greatest enemy or your greatest motivator. I talk to myself whenever thoughts enter my head of quitting or procrastinating due to fear. It is normal to feel fear when you lack the wisdom, relationships, or resources to bring your vision to past, but it does not mean that fear should be given permission to move in. Although, fear is a normal feeling I consistently speak positive words of affirmation over myself, family, friends, ministry, and businesses daily.

Winning is a decision, moving forward in spite of how you emotionally feel is a choice, and overcoming is about mind renewal. Shift the way you view your life, and you will shift the obstacles that weigh you down. It is possible to have peace in the middle of a storm in your life. People will not understand you because maintaining peace and rest is abnormal when trials arise, but it is possible. Mind renewal is a key to winning. Understanding the characteristics, attributes, and purpose of God, Jesus, and the Holy Spirit is a key to winning because of whose image you are made in. Knowing your purpose for being born and who you are assigned to help is a key to winning. Knowing that you were created to win is a key to avoid settling for less but choosing instead to win. When fear attempts to paralyze you remember God's promise mentioned in Isaiah 41:10:

> Fear not, for I *am* with you;
> Be not dismayed, for I *am* your God.
> I will strengthen you,
> Yes, I will help you,
> I will uphold you with My righteous right hand.'

We are not women of strength because we look to ourselves physically but because God sustains us through it all. Maybe you have experienced similar pains as I and if you have I commend you because you are still standing. These are just a few of many pains which temporarily affected me, but I eventually overcame them all. An in-depth version of my testimony is in chapter nine. Some of the pains that I overcame: being removed from my mother's home due to drugs resulting in me living in a group home for over three years, the victim of rape at the hands of my mother's friend's son, a lifestyle of sex and drug trafficking due to low self-esteem and not knowing who I was, the loss of a husband and mother unexpectedly, several close calls with death, and incarceration for several hours that could have led to years. I know that I do not look like what I have been through, that is the grace of God.

Before I decided to turn my life around and live a Godly lifestyle I experienced many things because of poor choices, bad associations, and out of ignorance. Once my mind was renewed I began on a road of growth and maturity that opened up new levels of issues but opportunities to overcome them. Your past is your past. I have learned to release it because my past is just that my past. Some pains are self-inflicted, caused by your own hands or actions, and some pains are a result of another's actions toward you. It does not matter how the pain entered your life, decide that it cannot reside with you any longer; give it an eviction notice.

Shift the way you view your life and you will shift the obstacles that weigh you down.

Prayer: Lord please forgive me for giving permission for pain to reside with me which has resulted in paralysis of my purpose. Lord You are my strength and I thank You for giving me the strength and wisdom to overcome every obstacle that has caused pain in my life. No longer will I look through the eyes of pain but rather the eyes of purpose as I move forward trusting in You to guide me to completion. Amen!

Have you given past pain or fear permission to paralyze your purpose? If so write down the day that YOU WILL DECIDE to evict them out of your life.

_____
_____
_____
_____
_____
_____

Daily meditation in God's Word will strengthen you from the inside out, eliminating the possibility of anything or anyone robbing you of your internal peace and power ever again. What steps will you take to maintain your peace and power?

_____
_____
_____
_____
_____
_____
_____

A servant leader is a person in service to another who leads. Do not believe the myth that leaders only delegate without assisting others. True leaders are servants. Your purpose and gift was created to serve others, do you know who you are called to serve as a servant leader?

_____
_____
_____
_____
_____
_____
_____
_____

Do you have an understanding of where your strength comes from? Explain.

_____
_____
_____
_____
_____
_____
_____
_____
_____

SIX

Possess Your Power

WITHIN EVERY WOMAN LIES THE POWER TO MOVE MOUNTAINS AND SHIFT ATMOSPHERES

You have been empowered to write the next chapter of your life. "For you shall remember the: Lord your God, for it is He that gives you power to get wealth…" (Deut 8:18). You have been empowered with wisdom, anointing, ideas, concepts, and strategies to get wealth for the sole purpose of fulfilling His will in the earth. To "Get" represents the ability to attract, create, and produce wealth; but remember that you must not forget the one who gave you the power to produce it.

Possess your power by activating the gifts, ideas, and anointing within you to create and attract that which you are passionate about by moving forward. Accessing your power is connected to the development of your potential. Potential is untapped ability that you have not experienced yet. A demand must be placed on your potential for the door of growth to open. To operate at a level that you have yet to experience requires faith, focus, determination, action, and perseverance. Faith...that God can expand your territory with the resources you presently have. Focus...to block out all distractions that would attempt to detour your path from purpose. Determination...that moves you through obstacles into open doors of opportunity. Action...that propels you into high levels of success. Perseverance...that motivates you to walk on top of everything that would attempt to walk on you. Success is like a flavorful recipe, you do not need everything to make the taste exquisite, you just need the right ingredients.

Accessing your power is connected to the development of your potential.

BE INTENTIONAL ON PURPOSE

Possessing your power must be intentional, it will not happen by accident nor will it happen because you complain about how hard life is. Whatever area you have been gifted to operate in requires continuous development and education. You do not have to necessarily go to a traditional school to develop your potential. There are additional educational tools provided by professionals such as specialized course studies, mentorship programs, workshops, and opportunities to connect with like-minded people known as mastermind groups. Are you empowering yourself by increasing your knowledge daily in your desired field whether it is business, ministry, motivational speaking, entertainment, etc.? Books and audio trainings should become a part of your daily regiment; feeding your mind will broaden your view and vision. The development of your vision is your responsibility. Even if you are presently developing your vision there is always more components to it.

  I have reiterated the power of intentionality on several occasions because only when you are intentional about your success in life will you discipline yourself to press forward on purpose. Women of purpose are women of power, producing results, and impacting the lives of all who have the privilege of encountering their presence. Your power is not external; it lies within you and reflects through the companies, ministries, and people you build.

  Although I encouraged you to develop your vision intentionally and put it into action, as God begins to elevate you, always remember that your worth is not in what you do or do not have. Your worth is not in who you know or even in how many educational degrees that you have hanging on your wall. Your worth is in understanding the one who imparted the gifts within you and the purpose of that gift. It is your responsibility to possess your power by positioning yourself to gain an understanding of who you are through understanding the One who created you. Everything you need is on the inside of you; learn how to bring what is on the inside of you into reality. There are people with external possessions who lack the understanding of who they really are therefore they live lives that lack power. You are a woman of power poised and postured to do more than what you are presently doing.

Your power is not external; it lies within you and reflects through the people you build.

YOUR SUCCESS IS ONE DECISION AWAY

"I think that I want to do sales and marketing, no maybe real-estate, how about I just get a job? What do I really want to do?" this is only one of many conversations that I have had with myself. When seeking direction from God trust that He will guide you. Whenever you try to pursue your personal plans over God's will for your life you open the door to confusion. Confusion leads to indecisiveness; indecisiveness can lead to years of delay, and delay will open the door to regret. Acquiring money and prestige alone is meaningless if you accomplish it apart from your passion, your purpose because it will leave you feeling empty. One of the purposes of this book is to inspire you to pursue your purpose and tap into your gift intentionally, while trusting God to direct you. Through obedience wealth will come not only financially but spiritually, socially, physically, and emotionally as well.

 I was a jack of all trades; busy doing much but accomplishing very little. It is only when I began praying to God about my specific gifts and His designed purpose for my life that my desire for just occupying my time changed. I later learned that talent and giftedness are two different things. You may be talented at writing but gifted at inspiring people. You may be talented at singing but gifted at developing businesses and mentoring entrepreneurs. Regardless of what it is understand the difference between having a talent and operating in your area of giftedness. Your gift is connected to your passion that flows from your purpose. When you are passionate about something your heart beats for it. You are willing to build it without pay if necessary, although you will not have to. I will explain in further detail profiting tips in chapter eight "Turn Your Passion into Profits." You are literally one decision away from the life that you have envisioned but you must not limit your potential within.

 I am often asked how am I able to start a company based on the vision that I had or exemplify the boldness to travel to a business strategy event alone if necessary? The first step to activating your gift is making a conscious decision that you will. Every action begins with a decision. Faith is not having everything in place before you move, faith is taking what you have and trusting the one who gave you the vision to guide you and multiply your efforts as you move forward in obedience. God operates outside human understanding. Please do not misunderstand me, faith alone will not work; you must apply your hands to something and implement both practical and spiritual principles to produce extra-ordinary results while in peace.

One decision led to the birthing of a vision that was given to me not long ago. Kingdom Entrepreneurs International, LLC (KEi) was started in June 2012, four months after I originally received the vision of what the companies name and purpose would be. Out of fear I delayed being that I, in my finite mind, was trying to figure out how God would bring this vision to past being that I did not have the connections, resources, or wisdom to do so. After moving forward and establishing KEi's first Kingdom Entrepreneurial Business and Leaders Impact conference on October 13, 2012 I discovered that if I would only trust Him He would provide on every spectrum needed. Favor, resources, workers, wisdom, and attendees showed up not because I had faith one hundred percent of the time but because God was faithful to meet me as I **moved forward** while at times wondering how it was going to be possible.

Just because you cannot see beyond your limitations does not mean that you should not move forward by faith. But understand that God is not limited by your limitations, and He will honor your obedience to move forward. I did it, and you can to. God is faithful.

I must admit, I am so extremely grateful for that opportunity to grow; my faith has increased tremendously because of it. Our Ladies of Royalty Impact Women's Business & Empowerment Conference (www.LadiesofRoyalty.com) was birth shortly thereafter due to the birthing of the initial vision of Kingdom Entrepreneurs International, LLC. You have been given the power to choose. When it concerns living a beyond average lifestyle you have two choices to decide from: to trust God and believe that He has already empowered you to succeed or you can accept your current situation as the climax of your life's story. Your best life is one decision away.

POSITION YOUR POWER

Have you ever heard the saying after something great happened to you that it was because you were at the right place at the right time. Experiencing the fullness of your purpose is about positioning. I cannot drive this home enough, positioning your power begins with making the decision that you will not disrespect yourself by attempting to be someone else.

Understanding your worth and embracing your gifts will keep your mind alert and distant from the illusion of wanting to be as someone else. I entered the world of "ethical" business in 2002 that opened the door to a world of possibilities. I purposely put emphasis on ethical because in my distant past the business that I transacted was far from ethical; I thank God for freeing me from a life of bondage. In this new world of business I was introduced to both men and women winning intentionally. They were goal setters and standard makers. Time management, leadership development, and winning were a philosophy that they had adopted because they had possessed their power. My associations and environment played an important role in cultivating the gifts hidden within me. Within every woman lies the potential to become....become that public speaker that she has always wanted to be, complete that college degree, start that business, launch that ministry, or write that book.

Positioning your power begins with making the decision that you will not disrespect yourself by attempting to be someone *else*.

Potential is inactive ability that can be paralyzed by fear if it is given permission to take the place of faith. Fear opens the door to confusion, which leads to procrastination that can result in the aborting of your vision. Whether you are presently in business or aspiring to start one, it is time to position your purpose by possessing your power. You can position personally your purpose by tailoring your environment and association around your God given visions and gifts. Negative environments plus negative associations equals negative manifestations. Productive environments plus productive associations equals productive manifestations.

EXPECT TO WIN

What is your expectancy level? Do you expect to win? Do you even believe that you are worthy to be used? While attending my home church Pastor Michael D Moore made a statement so profound but true, "Just because it looks like you are losing does not mean that you are." That is a statement that I have adopted as a personal philosophy for my life. I occasionally repeat it whenever I want to encourage myself. Get in the habit of encouraging yourself; it is a great motivator for pressing forward in the midst of a storm, fear, or doubt.

Expectancy is to look for the arrival of something greater than good; it is a bold posture of knowing that whatever you are expecting is on its way. Whatever you expect from your actions of faith will produce eventually. Do YOU believe that? Critics may challenge that statement with their intellectual opinions but faith has little to do with intellect. Faith is about acting on the word of God that you believe. Faith is when you pursue your dreams, your visions, out of an act of obedience before everything that you think you need is available. Acting out of intellect alone is not faith. Mix wisdom with faith, and you have an explosive combination.

Actions always follow faith. I have ignorantly said that I had faith on several occasions but lacked the action required that would qualify it as faith. I encourage you to do an in-depth study on what action faith is versus hope. To boldly declare that you are knowledgeable about a thing but lack the knowledge to understand why you are doing it can be defined as ignorance. Ignorance is not a derogatory word; it just simply means that you did not know. Words have power and the words that you speak over your life will paint the canvas of your life.

Action always follows faith.

PRAYER: Lord Thank You for empowering me to possess my power and position my purpose. Forgive me for devaluing my purpose by trying to be someone or do something outside of Your will for my life. Thank You for giving me the wisdom to understand the difference between a talent vs my gift. May all that I do and build be connected to Your will and Your way. Amen!

What does the next chapter of your life look like?

_____
_____
_____
_____
_____
_____
_____

Accessing your power is connected to the development of your potential. What steps are you presently taking to develop your potential?

_____
_____
_____
_____
_____
_____
_____
_____
_____

Are you empowering yourself by increasing your knowledge daily in your desired field? Explain.

_____
_____
_____
_____
_____

_____
_____
_____

Your best life is ONE DECISION away. What does that statement mean to you?

_____
_____
_____
_____
_____
_____
_____

Expectancy is to look for something greater than good. What is your expectancy level? Do you expect to win?

_____
_____
_____
_____
_____
_____
_____
_____

SEVEN

Average Just Won't Do

YOU POSSES THE POWER WITHIN
TO REWRITE YOUR LIFE'S SCRIPT?

There is good and then there is great; there are ordinary accomplishments then there are extraordinary accomplishments. There is average and then there is YOU: exceptionally gifted beyond that of average. Have you ever had a project that you were responsible for completing, whether it was for school, work, or business that you gave one hundred percent of your efforts to? Once complete your project's outcome was above mediocrity only because your main focus from the start was to produce extraordinary results. A mindset of excellence will set the course for the ultimate outcome. Working with an attitude of excellence is not limited or reserved for a project or goal only, this is who you are...you are extraordinary, a Woman of Excellence.

Average is just that....average; nothing worth making a fuss over and nothing worth discussing. When you operate ABOVE-average you force the world to pay attention. A mind-set that operates above-average is one that is EXTRAordinary. Dictionary.com defines extraordinary as one who is beyond what is usual or regular; exceptional in character; remarkable. The mere fact that we as women were created in the very image of God who created the entire universe and everything in it should be the motivating factor behind why we will live a life BEYOND what is ordinary.

When you operate ABOVE-average you force the world to pay attention.

I am confident in saying that at some point in your life you have felt unworthy, average, rejected, or inferior due to lies that you may have believed directed at yourself or because of failures that you may have made. Regardless of the reason, you epitomize the essence of what defines EXTRAordinary. You may not see it at the moment, you may not feel it internally, but it is in you to produce something above the norm.

Madam C.J. Walker was an extraordinary woman of vision who as an African American defied the norm by becoming America's first female self-made millionaire in the early 1900s because of her business success in the hair care industry. How was it that a woman who was looked upon as inferior by society in a world of prejudice could build an extraordinary company, along with beauty schools during such dire times? She refused to limit her vision despite the odds against her. She did not allow society to shape her world; she took responsibility and participated in shaping her own success. You must participate in your own success. Whereas, God is empowered to work on your behalf as you walk in obedience by faith, He is also limited by any doubt, inaction, or lack of faith. It is very important that you understand YOU MUST PARTICIPATE IN YOUR OWN SUCCESS.

You MUST participate in your own success.

WHY SETTLE FOR LESS

While attending a business conference the keynote speaker invited you to the front of the room and pulled out a $100 dollar bill along with a $50 dollar bill then proceeded by asking you a question, "If I gave you the choice of choosing the dollar amount that you would walk away with what would you choose?" Now I propose a similar question to you, what dollar amount would you have chosen: the $100 or $50 dollar bill? This is an amazing example of how we can limit ourselves based on the choices that we make.

I have done this analogy on several occasions while speaking to groups of insightful individuals and without fail the chosen person has always chosen the $100 dollar bill over the $50. You may be thinking at this very moment that you would have also done the same because the $100 is twice as much as the $50 dollar bill but the question that was asked was, "If I gave you the choice of choosing the dollar amount that you would walk away with what would you choose?" If you were given the choice of choosing why not choose both the $100 dollar bill along with the $50 dollar bill for a total of $150 dollars. Choosing the amount that you perceived to be larger actually limited you by $50 dollars; you where previously empowered with the choice to choose both but neglected to do so. The outcome was determined by how you perceived the question that was asked and the value of the choices you were given.

Perception plays an important role in the decision making process. To perceive is to become aware of or identify by means of senses. How you perceive a thing will determine your actions toward it, which includes yourself. Your perception of yourself will also determine the limitations that you will or will not allow to hinder you from moving toward your dreams and visions. Once you see yourself as an overcomer, gifted, and forgiven by God for any errors that you may have made in the past you will refuse to be bound by any limiting force, challenge, or person. You will never ever again settle for anything less than God's best not because you are so great but because God is and you, the W.O.M.A.N., are made in His image.

How you perceive a thing will determine your actions toward it, which includes yourself.

PERFECTION VS EXCELLENCE

As a woman in pursuit of purpose whether building a business, starting a ministry, writing a book, managing a team of people, or running a corporation understanding the difference between perfectionism and excellence is key to development. Perfectionism sounds like something that should be acquired when in essence perfection is not what you should desire but rather excellence. Perfectionism has been known to stop the greatest creators and innovative thinkers due to their inability to move pass one point to the next. There are stages to growth called the Law of Process; if you get stuck at a stage it could cost you precious time, energy, and possibly money. There is a very familiar saying that practice makes perfect when in actuality practice does not make perfect it makes you better. The fact that CHANGE is inevitable reminds us that anything deemed as perfect will soon be enhanced. Do not fall into the trap of society that you are not great until you have achieved perfection because perfection should not be your ultimate goal but rather excellence.

Those who strive for excellence versus perfectionism desire to operate at their highest and best ability. Operating with an attitude of excellence will result in limited excuses, timely execution in getting a task completed, and above average results. As a little girl I have always had the desire to strive for more and not settle. Once I entered the world of business in 2002 I got my first taste of what attempting to create perfection felt like: stress, anxiety, frustration, worry, lack of peace, and incomplete results. Nothing was ever good enough. Out of ignorance I would complain about how difficult it was to accomplish a goal while placing such unrealistic expectations on myself that prevented me from ever attaining them. I literally lost years of time for no other reason than trying to get the task just right before I moved to the next phase.

Only when I developed in my thinking was I able to move forward toward progress. This book is a great example of my desire to provide to my readers quality material and information in a spirit of excellence versus perfectionism. This book was written from my heart, from my life experiences, and as I felt lead by God. Whatever you do give it your best effort without placing unrealistic expectations on yourself.

Only when I transitioned in my thinking was I able to move forward toward progress.

YOU ARE WHAT YOU THINK

Never settle for less than God's best. Pray before you make a decision to do anything; just because it is a good thing does not make it a God thing. When your plans are connected to God's will for your life you will have the boldness, faith, and tenacity to overcome the voice within you that desires to partner with mediocrity. When you decide to walk in your power expect a battle in your mind to surface. The enemy desires to stop you with tactics to convince you to meditate on lies versus truth. If your thought of meditation leads to weariness and pain you must take authority over that thought by encouraging yourself through positive affirmations, reading the word of God, or listening to positive messages on CD. Meditation is good because it allows you to posture your mind for progress.

Meditation is good because it allows you to posture your mind for progress.

Have you ever wondered what your true thoughts were about yourself? Take an inventory or assessment of how you really see or feel about yourself; not how someone else feels or thinks but how you personally see yourself. How do you see yourself: is it empowering or degrading to your self-worth; is it encouraging or feeds on the insecurity within you? What do you personally think about yourself? As an athlete in high school I would get challenged by team members who believed they were more competitive than I. Although, I was very tiny I viewed myself as having more heart and determination therefore my actions lined up with the thoughts that I had toward myself. Your life will not develop beyond your own perception of yourself.

    If you are dealing with insecurity, low self-esteem, shyness, procrastination, fear, anything that would threaten to rob you of your power as a woman I encourage you to purchase, read, and meditate on books that would empower you. The books that I recommend, starting with the Holy Bible, are designed to help you break free from the bondages mentioned above. There are books that specialize specifically in particular areas for example "Battlefield of the Mind" by Joyce Meyer is a great book for both men and women constantly warring in their minds. Whether the books are spiritual or personal development books there are several reputable authors who have contributed to my personal development as a woman of purpose and power. I am an advocate reader in the areas of spiritual and practical material but my number one book to read is the Holy Bible. I grew to understand that if I was not knowledgeable of the One who created me in His image and why, how would I ever know the true value that I carry within.

<blockquote>Your life will not develop beyond your own perception of yourself.</blockquote>

Do not be deceived. No amount of compliments in the world will ever compare to you complimenting yourself once you know your true worth. This is not arrogance this is confidence. There will be days when there is no one to encourage you; will you be able to encourage yourself? Will you be able to continue in your quest in building a legacy of greatness? You are what you meditate on. Thoughts of poverty will lead to a life of mediocrity. Thoughts of creativity, impacting lives, and abundance will lead to the development of something great and life transforming. It is your responsibility to develop in your thinking through reading and meditating on that which you desire to become.

Prayer: Thank You Father for reminding me that living an average lifestyle is not Your best plan for my life. Lord I thank You for giving me the wisdom and strength to operate at a level of excellence that far exceeds my own ability. May I never limit You because of any personal limitations that I may have. I choose to believe what You have said about me, yes I am beautifully and wonderfully made, and You have blessed and empowered me to dominate in the earth for Your glory. Amen!

What does operating in a mind-set of excellence mean to you?

_____
_____
_____
_____
_____
_____

Are you making the necessary action steps to participate in your own success? How? If not when?

_____
_____
_____
_____
_____
_____

Has perfectionism held you back? If so, why is it important to direct your focus toward achieving excellent results versus perfect results?

_____
_____
_____
_____

_____
_____
_____

How do you see yourself: is it empowering or degrading to your self-worth; is it encouraging or does it feed on the insecurity within you? What is your perception of yourself?

_____
_____
_____
_____
_____
_____
_____
_____

How often do you compliment yourself? Write five compliments that you will consistently say to yourself?

_____
_____
_____
_____
_____
_____
_____
_____

EIGHT

You Are a Woman of Wealth

WHAT IS LIFE WITHOUT PEACE? ......MISERY

Wealth…..what is it? If I were to take a survey the majority of people answering this question would limit wealth to money or possessions. Even the dictionary limits wealth to material possessions, monetary gain, and assets. Although true wealth does include money and possessions, it is not limited to them. True wealth is peace and wholeness in these five areas of life: spiritual, social, physical, financial, and emotional. Whereas, you will most likely devote more time to one area more than the others valuing all five areas is key to living a fulfilling life of wealth.

SPIRITUAL wealth sets the course for the other four areas that encompasses the whole of your life. We all have either had a personal relationship with or have met "externally" successful people who have the money, prestige, influence but are sick in their bodies, minds, relationships, or spiritual life. When you intentionally develop a relationship with your creator, God, the one who privileged you with the gifts, talents, creativity, and ideas to acquire success it produces a high level of peace that can weather any life storm. Growing spiritually is a challenge for many building companies or taking on multiple tasks, but it is possible. As a woman of wealth God must be in the center of every decision or plan you make. Just like you would make an appointment with clients or family, make it a goal to make an appointment to meet with Him daily: prayer, reading, meditation, and fellowship will keep you balanced spiritually. Eventually this discipline will become a habit that you cannot live without.

As a woman of wealth God must be in the center of every decision or plan you make.

SOCIAL wealth results from developing promising and thriving relationships, starting with family, friends, and colleagues. Cultivating your relationships plays a vital role in the level of peace you will experience. Whenever you neglect family, spouse or children, you eat away at your peace which hinders the proper development of you becoming socially wealthy. Other relationships are very important: family in addition to spouse, children, friends, spiritual and business mentors, colleagues, employees, and clients. This is not an exhaustive list but certain relationships require a higher level of importance. Remember love and appreciation is shown not just spoken.

PHYSICAL wealth allows you the luxury of enjoying other areas of wealth. What is money without health? There are certain illnesses that money cannot cure, only the power of God. Making health a top priority in your life can be the difference between life or death, living healthy or handicapped. This area of wealth is dear to my heart because I lost my husband in 2002 and my dear mother in 2008 due to health related issues that was a result of poor eating habits. Sadly enough many diseases are self-inflicted due to poor diets. It is a statistical fact that many of the diseases that we face today are largely due to poor diets: poor nutrition, too much sugar, processed foods, not enough natural foods in our diets, fast foods, large consumption of cigarettes, alcohol, and a lack of exercise. Must I continue? Wealth in any area is intentional. You have been empowered to make the decision that your life is worth living.

FINANCIAL wealth is the ability to create an abundant supply of resources: monetary, assets, and possessions. Being financially wealthy affords you the ability to live in opulence and affluence. It is amazing how many people desire financial wealth but refuse to increase their financial knowledge to acquire and manage it, take action steps toward its development, or educate themselves in the area of investing. Being rich and financially wealthy will put you in two totally different spectrums in life. Wealth is connected to legacy; it transfers from one generation to the next. Riches can wither away within one generation from a bad investment. Wealth should not be created only for your generational lineage but for the legacy of schools, ministries, businesses, and foundations you can build or donate into and for the people you can impact far after you have passed on. Financial wealth gives you the ability to make decisions that others can only complain about or hope for.

    EMOTIONAL wealth is priceless. The true definition of success is emotional peace and freedom in your mind and spirit. Knowing your worth as a woman, understanding who God is and why He chose to create you in His image, and walking in your purpose are door openers to a level of uncommon peace. Just because trials, test, and challenges arise does not mean that you have to allow them to rob you of your peace of mind. Your emotions should always be at a calm state. Whenever you are emotionally stressed, depressed, or worried sickness is on the verge of developing. Statistically speaking depression can lead to death. Meditate on joyous things even in the midst of a painful situation. Envision the end result; try to see the good within every challenging obstacle. It may be tough, but it is possible to maintain your sanity and peace. What is freedom? Freedom is when you have freed yourself from the opinions of people and unrealistic expectations of yourself. Love yourself just the way you are at every level of development. We all are a beautiful work in progress.

> *Love yourself just the way you are at every level of development. We all are a beautiful work in progress.*

DOES BALANCE EXIST

The question is often asked, "Does balance exist and if so how do you balance everything simultaneously?" It depends on who you ask whether balance exist or not but my personal assessment is yes experiencing a balance life is possible.

I was recently at a business conference and the "balance" question was asked to the speaker who replied, "No, balance does not exist." Same question different conference. I recently hosted a business and leaders conference and the "balance" question was asked; the speaker reply, "You may not be able to give every area the same amount of attention but balance is possible when you put whatever you are doing at that moment priority over the other areas." He gave an example, "When you are at church focus on church, do not try to solicit for business. When you are spending time with family, do not attempt to answer business calls. When you are handling business do not waste time with friends on idol conversation." He made some great eye opening points that eliminated the excuse of husbands and wives not having time for their child or each other because of work, business, or ministry obligations. His point of view placed value on every area of life as we scheduled it.

I enjoy listening to others view on balance, it is so intriguing. My interpretation, balance is how you define it based on the priorities that you have in your life of importance. A woman who is married has a different responsibility than a single woman, just as a businesswoman has a different responsibility than an employee. Your balance is determined by you not anyone else who lives outside of your world of priorities.

YOUR HEALTH IS A PART OF YOUR WEALTH

As mentioned earlier, health allows you the luxury of enjoying the other areas of your life. I am not a doctor or physician but I do know that America is consumed by food and the microwave mentality of I must have it right now. I live down south in a state that ranks among the highest in obesity - type two diabetes in children is continuously rising, and there are more heart attacks than ever before, to name a few.

I do not claim to be the healthiest eater but I have made a conscious decision to remove certain foods from my diet to decrease my chances of self-inflicting health issues. Too much of anything can be bad for you but not enough of some foods also can be bad for you. Water for instance, not drinking enough water can lead to many health issues. Raw vegetables are great for the body as is sugars can work against the body. I encourage you to research further on the foods and drinks that promote good health and also those that can work against your health.

Food and drink are not the only components to living a strong and healthy lifestyle. Experts also highlight the importance of rest, exercise, a daily dose of fresh air and sunshine, maintaining a mind free from worry, and time set aside just to think. Your health is worth educating yourself and applying what you learn. Poor habits toward your body over a consistent period of time can lead to cancer, high blood pressure, diabetes, high cholesterol, obesity, etc. My mother carried many of these diseases not because they were hereditary but because she consumed pork, fried foods, and cases of sodas daily. She also woke in the middle of the night for years to eat cookies, along with smoking packs of cigarettes daily. Much as I loved my mother she played an enormous role in the diseases that surfaced in her life as a result of her neglect toward her body. My husband's life was cut short due to a massive heart-attack because he refused to follow the doctor's order of cutting back salts and certain foods to lose weight. We do play a major role in how our bodies are affected by illnesses.

BUILD A LASTING LEGACY

Your success in your spiritual, social, physical, financial, and emotional life is totally up to you. Whether you agree or disagree you are the co-creator of your life, God is the creator. You cannot move forward into purpose until you first take responsibility of your own actions or inactions. There are people depending on you and your gifts to set them free from the bondage that they have lived with for years but how can you set them free if you are bound as well. Whatever ails you release it, ask God for the wisdom and strength to overcome every obstacle that have stood in your way. Remember, within your DNA is the ability to help meet a need where voidance exist. Refuse to agree with your present circumstances because if you do you will remain stuck in that moment of stagnation.

Legacy is something that you leave purposefully to past down to the next generation. Let your legacy not be limited to money and possessions but impact and purpose. May the children of your children tell stories of how you valued life and not only money; how you were purpose driven and due to your determination the world is a better place because of it. May you teach people what an example of a worry free lifestyle looks like; may you talk more through your actions than your words. May you be known as the W.O.M.A.N in your family who defied the odds, overstepped boundaries, conquered adverse situations, and created what others viewed as impossible.

Perfection is not what we strive for but rather excellence in every area of our lives. You define what balance means to you and commit to making it a lifestyle. You are a woman of wealth: one who is successful in her relationship with God, relationship with family and friends, health, finances, and mental stability. May you take control of your life, understanding that you do play a part in the birthing process of your destiny. God is the creator and you have been given delegated authority to co-create your world; the power of your success is determined by your daily decisions.

Let your legacy not be limited to money and possessions but impact and purpose.

Prayer: Lord thank You for giving me the wisdom and insight to know the importance of living a wealthy life in my spiritual walk with You, relationships, health, finances, and emotions. Forgive me Lord for neglecting any area of my life that was of importance. Father God I ask You to give me the divine strength and wisdom to steward every area of my life in excellence for Your glory. Amen!

What steps must you take or habits must you break to put God in the center of your life?

_____
_____
_____
_____
_____
_____

Wealth is not limited to money although it includes it. What area of your life do you desire to become more fruitful in: spiritual, relational, physical, financial, and/or emotional? Why?

_____
_____
_____
_____
_____
_____

What is your plan of action for achieving this desire of fruitful progression?

_____
_____
_____
_____
_____

In any area of life the power of your success is determined by your daily decisions. What ONE decision will you make today that will lead you on a path toward success? Why is this decision important to your success?

NINE

Turn Your Passion into Profit

EITHER YOU ARE WORKING YOUR VISION AS A
BUSINESS OR A HOBBY, BUT YOU CANNOT DO BOTH

There is an entrepreneur inside every woman; having the ability to take a creative vision or passion and turn it into a business or enterprise. While sitting at a business conference the speaker read a business statistic from 2011 that read, "In 2011 there were 2.6 million new millionaires created and 67 percent of them were women." My mouth dropped. I was so elated by that report that it motivated me even more into encouraging women to turn their passion into profits. The challenge that many women are having, and I once had, is we tend to work our gifts and passions as a hobby vs as a business. After years of this behavior mind renewal is necessary. As Pastor Sheryl Brady so powerfully stated at the 2012 Woman Thou Art Loosed conference with Bishop T.D. Jakes, "I can't be who I am and who I was at the same time." You cannot walk into your new identity holding on to your past habits.

> You cannot walk into your new identity holding on to your past habits.

What are you passionate about? Does this passion line up with your God designed purpose? Awareness plays a very important part in wise decision making. I have learned that if something does not line up with God's designed plan for my life I will give it no time or attention. Just because it is a good thing or it can make money does not make it purposeful for you. Whenever you work in your area of giftedness the money will come. Never allow the lust for money to lead you into making a business decision; it will cost you eventually, and the price may be your peace of mind.

Qualified I am when it comes to sharing the importance of working in your purpose. I spent years running after opportunities in pursuit of more money. I wasted countless years, energy, and money on businesses that I was not led to pursue. The great part about it all was I learned valuable lessons about decision making, leadership, team building, time management, and wise investing. Every business decision that I made was not unproductive but I found my greatest joy and peace when I began learning how to monetize my gifts intentionally. Do not be afraid of failing. Failure does not mean that you should never try again; instead you should gather the lessons learned from your failures then try again with more wisdom.

FOLLOW YOUR PASSION

What is it that drives you; that consumes your thinking and have you up at night? What is it that you do with little effort at all? What is it that convicts your heart to tears? Are you an encourager, inspirational speaker, writer, business developer? Are you a teacher, philanthropist, or minister? Are you an advocate for abused children or women, or are you an inventor of unique products? What is it that makes you unique from everyone else? You are your purpose; no one will be able to do you quite like you.

> You are your purpose; no one will be able to do you quite *like you.*

For years countless people have recognized my gift of speaking and unique way of motivating people but I would casual brush it off with a, "Yes I am aware of it, everyone tells me that." To be very transparent with you although I found joy in inspiring people the thought of speaking as a career or business terrified me. I am aware that fear played a major role in the passivity that I allowed to handicap me. Only after I accepted my

God designed assignment and began speaking to myself was I able to start developing systems to monetize my gifts of speaking and product development. One statement that I made to myself after accepting my assignment was, "Yakinea Marie God has graced you to build people, businesses, and products. Refuse to allow fear to hold you back. It is ok for you to turn your passion into profits." This was extremely liberating and life transforming for me. Even if you have to talk to yourself remind yourself of what your purpose is and why you must not quit.

MONETIZE YOUR GIFT

You should be earning income from what you are passionate about and if you are not it could be because you are viewing it as a casual hobby. To monetize your gift is to develop an income generating system from what you are passionate about. For example: if you are known for your famous sweet potato pies you want to develop a business plan and goal to creating revenue for your gift of baking. Depending upon how large your vision is you eventually could own a manufacturing and distribution company to your own pie enterprise. Women often limit their gifts because they view them as small or as a past-time hobby. Someone with vision could take that same concept and create a fortune with it. It is all about vision; how you view your creative abilities and understanding that fear will contaminate your vision.

> *You should be earning income from what you are passionate about.*

Fear is a paralyzing emotion that has a subtle way of convincing you that you do not have what it takes; no one will purchase anything from you, besides you would not know how to operate a business anyway. Lies! Lies! Lies! The illusion that you cannot accomplish a task is indeed a lie from the enemy. We are reminded that WITH GOD "nothing" will be impossible. Do you believe that? What you truly believe will manifest in your life. Belief is not just words but action. If you believe then begin the process of researching the How To's to starting a business, marketing and monetizing your gift, and the industry your purpose is connected to. Do not wait. Educating yourself and becoming more versed on your product or idea is an intentional action of faith.

YOUR PURPOSE WILL PRODUCE PROFITS

"A man's gift (which includes a women's gift) makes room for him, and brings him before great men". (Proverbs 18:16) Your gift has been given the assignment to make room and open doors for you; to connect you to people of prominence and influence. You do not have to make room for your gift because God has assigned your gift to make room for you. To make room is the opening of many doors of opportunity and favor for your gift to be seen. You should be in high expectation that your gift is making room for you, even at this very moment. Developing and expanding in business is not just a natural experience but a spiritual one as well and you should desire to be like no one else on the earth other than who you have been created to be.

Desiring to be as someone else in business or life will distort the possibility and uniqueness of what can be done through you. Be the best at what you do. Ask yourself, "What makes me unique from the rest? How can I be different? How can I add more value to what I am offering?" Standing out may not be always comfortable, but it will brand you as a stand-alone entity of uniqueness. Chick-Fil-A, my favorite fast food restaurant, has uniquely branded themselves as having the friendliest customer service in the fast food industry. The chicken sandwich is great but the customer service is priceless. "How may I serve you?" is the one question that gives them the edge on other fast food chains. They also have uniquely branded themselves as a six day operation, closing on Sundays to give themselves and their employee's time for God and family. What makes you unique? What are you willing to sacrifice temporarily to obtain a permanent reward?

While working a traditional job sometimes 60 to 80 hours per week I would work part-time in my business. Why? Because I know that entrepreneurship is my purpose. I made the conscious decision that I would not allow a paycheck to detour me from positioning my gift to make room from me. While in the process of completing this book I made the decision to leave my job and pursue my God given purpose full-time by faith. My last day was February 1, 2013. I trust God for the ideas, creative strategizes and resources to do what He has created and tailored me to do as a W.O.M.A.N. in the earth. Obstacles may come but I will not give up on my dreams, goals, and who I am. May you do more in this next season of your life than you ever have, and may you refuse to allow limitations to hinder you from walking in the fullness of your divine purpose on purpose.

> May you do more in this next season of your life than you ever have, and may you refuse to allow limitations to hinder you from walking in the fullness of your divine purpose.

Prayer: Father God I am extremely grateful that You have gifted me to do great things in the earth. Lord I ask You to give me the wisdom, ideas, creative strategies, and resources to monetize my purpose. I declare that my gift is making room for me and is opening up doors of uncommon favor, resources, and influence. Lord may You be glorified through all that I do. Amen!

Are you working your passion as a hobby or business? If as a hobby, why? If as a business, are you maximizing your passion by growing your entity annually? How? If not, why?

_____
_____
_____
_____
_____
_____
_____
_____

Self-awareness will expose the enemy. Have you allowed fear to stagnate your gift and creativity? Are you hiding behind excuses? If so why?

_____
_____
_____
_____
_____
_____

What makes you unique from the rest? How can you add value to what you are presently offering?

_____
_____
_____
_____
_____

Write down five goals that you will accomplish in the next five years?

_____
_____
_____
_____
_____
_____
_____

What are you willing to sacrifice to gain a permanent reward?

_____
_____
_____
_____
_____

TEN

From Exotic Dancer to Executive
A Woman Who Overcame

**DON'T ALLOW YOUR PAST
TO SET THE COURSE FOR YOUR FUTURE**

    Wouldn't it be amazing if all children had the fortunate experience of growing up with both a loving and nurturing mother and father? Wouldn't it be a priceless emotional experience if all children felt that they were not secondary to their mother's or father's work, ministry, or addiction? Wouldn't it be beautiful if no child every experienced rape, molestation, mental, verbal, or physical abuse? Emotionally and personally what would life have been like if you as a child were prepared, nurtured, and positioned for life's challenges before adulthood? The great news is you still have an opportunity to rise above any challenge that has held you captive, imprisoned within your soul.

The substance of the question determines the power within the answer. I asked the previous thought provoking questions from a child's perspective because it is at the age of innocence that our philosophies and habits began to take root. It sets the course of our thinking, doing, and becoming.

Fifteen years has pasted and she is still allowing the wound of abuse as a teenager to affect her relationships as an adult. Twenty years has past and she still identifies herself as the woman who lacks self-worth because no one loved her as a child. Ten years has pasted, life is moving forward and things are going good but she lives in fear of embarrassment from the immoral and illegal things that she once did. Regardless of what it is, are you holding on to anything that would threaten your present peace or future fulfillment? We do not live in a perfect world but we have been given the power to choose. Yes, we all have made decisions that were not favorable to us but growth overtime motivated us to make wiser decisions. Although the odds may be stacked against you, I know from personal experience that when you have a heart to win life will start aligning on your behalf.

I have grown through a very challenging past. Without fail every time I share my testimony people often say to me, "You do not look like what you have been through." That statement is true even for you, "You do not look like what you have been through; you wear **VICTORY** well." We all have a testimony or story that depicts our road from victim to victor, being bound by the traumas of life that resulted in temporary paralysis. Notice I said "temporary" because when it is your desire to fight back it is a matter of time before you bounce back. It is truly stated that God does fight our battles but we have a responsibility to believe, see by faith, speak life, and act on what we believe. Believe that He is fighting on your behalf, look pass the pain and see yourself victorious, speak words of life that you desire to produce in your situation, and take action steps toward overcoming every obstacle.

You do not look like what you have been through;
you wear *Victory* well.

The testimony that I will share shortly will shock some and motivate others. I know that I was giving the grace to bounce back from a life of rape, separation from parents, drug trafficking, sexual promiscuity, criminal activities, loss of a husband and mother, business failures, and financial hardship so that I could serve and push other women of power to bounce back. There is NOTHING so powerful that God Himself cannot break from our lives, but we must be willing to admit that we need help.

Humility is a sign of strength. Be willing to give up your methods of fighting so that you can go up because of the one who is fighting on your behalf. I did not start healing within and winning in life until I became independent of man and dependent on God Himself. It does not matter who you think you are, your financial statement, your level of influence, your natural success in business if you have no relationship with the one who makes it all possible. LASTING STRENGTH comes from the one who gives it. I would not have had the mental strength to write this book today if I had not discovered the power of who I am in God.

THE BEGINNING...

No father figure, no example of what healthy love looked like, environment of drugs, victim of rape, scarcity of food, constant taunting by school kids and continuous fighting all before the age of 10 years old. A child of many dreams and visions; I often visualized myself as a truck driver until I saw a lady on television wearing a business suit, I quickly changed my goal to business ownership so that I to could wear a suit. In the third grade I was an entrepreneur selling candy to kids, but even back then I was not taught ethical and moral investing. I illegally withdrew coins from my mother's coin jar to finance my endeavor, which resulted in a painful spanking. It is funny now, but it was not funny then. After being disconnected from my mother and ultimately my siblings I began learning from foster parents what orderly living was and the meaning of discipline and rewards. I resided at the United Methodist Children Home

(UMCH) in Selma, Alabama for more than three years. As the years progressed I battled with many issues of rejection, low self-esteem, and insecurity that led me down a path of destruction, but it did not destroy me. It was there at UMCH, that the seed of competitiveness and open possibilities were born.

I did not start healing within and winning in life until I became independent of man and dependent on God Himself.

PROTECT THE INTERGRITY OF WHO YOU ARE

     Our past has the ability to predict our future only if we give it permission to; we have been given the power to choose. As an adult I eventually chose to turn my life in a positive direction: I changed occupations, went back to college, disconnected from negative associations, and worked toward building a stronger relationship and understanding of who God, Jesus, and the Holy Spirit was. It was not always that way. Once I arrived back to Birmingham from Selma, started my 11th grade year in high school, participated in athletics, and felt unstoppable I still became like so many teenagers, a pregnant mom at the age of 17.

     I have always had a strong drive to succeed despite the obstacles. Although, I was sick the entire nine months I was determined not to drop out of school. I went on to graduate with honors, and the rest is…..not history. My life spiraled downhill fast because I did not have the wisdom or courage to protect the integrity of who I was. I went from graduating with honors, to a college student, to connecting with the wrong people, which led me to a life of exotic dancing aka stripping, to drug trafficking because I did not protect the integrity of who I was. Admittedly I was ignorant, easily influenced, and blinded by a life of fast money.

Maybe you have never done anything immoral or illegal in your life that you can remember. Maybe you made all the right decisions: never smoked drugs (although I was never a drug user because of a promise I made to myself after seeing my mom's addiction), maybe you have never gotten drunk, nor had sexual intercourse outside of marriage. Just maybe you have never gossiped, been jealous of another's blessing, used profanity, or told a lie. Did I mention that maybe you have never procrastinated, poorly spent money, made excuses, been indecisive, or complained ungratefully. Maybe you have or have not, only you know. The purpose for my previous statements is no one is void of imperfection regardless of how they may be looked upon. Self-awareness is vital to living a life of freedom; identifying what it is that is attempting to poison your identity and contaminate your purpose.

> Our past has the ability to predict our future only if we give it permission to; we have been given the power to choose.

    Refuse to allow shame to prevent you from sharing what God has delivered you from. If you have done anything that once robbed you of your time, energy, money, peace, or self-worth and are able to live as a bold overcomer I encourage you to utilize your testimony and gift as a catalyst to assist others with entering a life of freedom. Remember, you do not owe anyone an explanation if someone tries to judge who you were. Always remember who you are and whose you are. The last two years of my street life consisted of my dancing at a strip club as well as going to church. Although, the last two years of my life was a battle between light and darkness the light that illuminated from The Light House Full Gospel Church began to chip away at the prison bars that I had given myself permission to reside behind. Prior to me being released from that lifestyle I began praying, asking God to help me find a way out of the streets.

    Whenever I can I express the gift of love to anyone that I see imprisoned to a life of immorality. I have learned that it is your love not your judgment that attracts those who may be praying quietly for someone to help them out of a life of bondage. As a woman of purpose: entrepreneur, minister, professional, wife, mother, student let your life speak for you. I am currently a minister, entrepreneur, CEO, life coach, author, and leader not because of what I went through but because of what I was willing to come out of.

PROTECT YOUR DREAMS, PROTECT YOUR PURPOSE

From the third grade I knew that I was born to be an entrepreneur. I did not understand the totality of it but in my heart I had already made up in my mind that I eventually would follow that path. The innocence of a child is so pure and authentic without precepts or inconsistencies. Children have the boldness to dream and envision themselves living in a world that in reality seems impossible, so the parents may think. As a child I dreamed, and I dreamed big.

Do you have a dream or vision that you have not fulfilled? If the answer is yes, have you identified what has led to your delay? Did someone tell you that you were not qualified, he or she would not support you, and you are insane for attempting such vision? Were you delayed by unexpected life tragedies that left you feeling overwhelm and depleted? Are you waiting for the affirmation of someone whose opinion you highly respect and refuse to get started until he or she approve? Has fear of the unknown paralyzed you? What is it that would threaten such a gift from being utilized in the earth by humanity? Some day you may say, but that day will never arrive if you continue to allow inner emotions or the issues of others to set your time of arrival for accomplishing your dream.

We all have been there, well at least I have: setting goals, writing plans, praying for it to be successful, taking CASUAL action only to result in little to no fruit. I have felt stuck, been delayed, and experienced stagnation over a long period of time because I made the error of accepting it as normal. There is nothing normal about operating at a level below what you were initially created for. Humans make errors in their creations but God does not.

There is nothing normal about operating at a level below what you were initially created for.

Environment is everything. Remaining in a negative environment makes it that much tougher to maintain a positive attitude and persevere despite the odds. It is your responsibility to protect your dreams, visions, and gifts. There are several ways to protect your purpose:

- ❖ Build your strength through meditating in God's Word
- ❖ Cover your visions and purpose in daily prayer
- ❖ Educate and inspire yourself through continuous reading and listening to personal development and inspirational materials
- ❖ Look for affirmation from God versus man

- ❖ Associate with others pursuing purpose as well
- ❖ Verbally confess daily to yourself what your gift and purpose are and why you would be a blessing to others
- ❖ Review your goals daily to remind yourself where you are goal and why you must not stopped.
- ❖ Develop a plan of action to accomplishing your goals
- ❖ Take actions steps daily toward accomplishing what you envision
- ❖ Steward your time by saying no to invitations that would waste it
- ❖ Refuse to listen to or accept any advice or comments from naysayers or critical people, including your family or friends.

It is possible to be married to or be friends with someone who does not support your vision or purpose. If this is the case do not make things worse by trying to argue with them or play the begging or convincing game. You can listen to those you love who are critical, who do not believe in you, and still maintain your peace. Practice replying to critical loved ones in a loving way and if married maintain unity with your husband through praying and believing God for unity of purpose. There is power when a husband and wife are on one accord; protect the unity in your marriage.

When critical opinions surface you do not have to participate with rebuttals or murmuring. Just because you choose not to rebut what they are saying does not mean that you have to receive their comments or advice. If someone says something contrary to what you believe just simply thank them for their advice then continue forward; under no circumstances should you try to convince anyone to see what God has implanted inside you. Taking this approach will keep you out of bitterness, frustration, or stagnation but rather in a posture of peace and expectation. Your gift will make room for you. As you pursue purpose doors of favor will open and those who once doubted you will desire to help you. Protect your peace; do not give anyone permission to take it.

> **Protect your peace; do not give anyone permission to take it.**

I AM AN OVERCOMER

An overcomer....that I am, and you are to. Who am I that God loves me enough to keep me from death, disease, and jail while in a life of immorality? After turning my life around 12 years ago who am I that God would sustain me even when I felt like giving up because of poverty, lack, and struggle as a single mother? Who am I that God would keep me in perfect peace after the death of my husband and mother? Who am I that

God would give me a second, third, fourth (who can count the times) opportunity to obey His instructions of stepping out by faith, trusting Him for the outcome? Who am I? I am a W.O.M.A.N. That is the same question that I propose to you…who are you that God would strengthen you to overcome that which tried to overcome you? Who are you that God would tailor you in His image? Who are you? You are a **W.O.M.A.N.** in pursuit of purpose: **W**onderful, **O**utstanding, **M**ade in His image, **A**nointed and **N**ot going to quit on your dreams.

    Your past pains do not have to be a part of your future successes. You were born to win: tailored for a purpose, postured for success, and empowered to prosper. An overcomer is one who has prevailed. You have been empowered to write the next chapter of your life. Do not wait on it to come, be intentional about fulfilling your purpose, go and get it. You epitomize the strength of a woman; one who was born to turn her pain into power.

You have been empowered to write the

next chapter of your life.

Prayer: Lord You are so faithful. Thank You for reminding me of who I am in You. Thank You for not holding my past against me because of Your forgiving love through Christ. Thank You for empowering me to win and for giving me the strength to overcome every pain, and every obstacle. Use me as a designer's original. Your will be done in my life. Amen!

Are you protecting the integrity of who you are, the real you? How?

_____
_____
_____
_____
_____
_____
_____

Do you have a life story to share that would deliver someone in a similar situation that you have not shared? Why haven't you shared your story? Are you still bound by it or man's opinion? Do you feel like you would be embarrassed if people knew what God had delivered you from? Remember, one of the ultimate freedoms that you will ever experience is when you GET FREE from man's opinion about you. They have NO power over you. Trust God and move forward. People are awaiting your arrival.

_____
_____
_____
_____
_____

Do you believe that you can? Do you believe that God will? Then what is your excuse?

Who are you that God would choose you for such a time as this?

ELEVEN

Fall in Love with Yourself

AN EXPRESSION OF LOVE THAT EMPOWERS

"I LOVE ME some me!" what a statement to make to yourself daily. If only we as women, God's Queen's, understood the power of loving ourselves as God does. If only we could see ourselves, not through the eyes of man or the eyes of our frailties but as God sees us; through the eyes of a Father's love.

Many women hate themselves and have no idea that they have become their own enemy. They crave the love of man (which includes woman) because they have been deceived into believing that they cannot move forward without another's approval, validation, or love. They feel as though they need another's love, but how can you truly express authentic love to someone unless you first love yourself? When you fall in love with yourself imagine the power that will be unlocked from within that will transfer outwardly empowering all whom you encounter. Authentic love...no unscrupulous or manipulative motive, just pure love. **STOP** for a moment and tell yourself just how much you love YOU. Even if you feel unworthy to be loved push through those negative feelings and tell yourself how much you love YOU.

Many women hate themselves and have no idea that they have become their own enemy.

Whenever you express love to yourself you increase your power within. A woman who truly loves herself will not settle for anything less than God's best; she refuses to lower her standards because she understands her power; she identifies herself through Christ and not through man's opinion of her; she is an authentic masterpiece of God's love. You may or may not agree but it is possible for you to love yourself. You are love because God is love; you have been created in His image and likeness.

Once upon a time I did not love myself. If you would have asked me years ago did I, I would have defensively replied, "What type of question is that, absolutely I love myself." Have you ever heard the statement actions speak louder than words? My actions were proof that I really did not truly love myself because I made decisions that were not in my best interest. The more you fall in love with yourself, from a God or forgiving perspective, the more your decisions will reflect that love. Seeing yourself as God does will eliminate guilt and condemnation; forgive yourself because He already has.

Whenever you express love to yourself you increase your power within.

ATTENTION!!!

Are you a selfish, self-consumed, prideful person? Do you make it a practice to focus on your needs over someone else? Have anyone ever made you feel like you are selfish because you chose to give attention to your need or desire over theirs. Do you buy into that guilt? Agree to eliminate the myth that you are selfish and prideful because you give attention to yourself. When life is all about you and only you then you have crossed the line of selfishness. However, balancing your needs within the framework of assisting others is selflessness.

Please do not misunderstand me; it is a wonderful feeling and act of love whenever you are willing to be the channel of blessing to someone in need despite your own needs. My goal is to differentiate between the two because women are so accustom to putting other's needs and desires before their own that they literally lose who they are in the process. As a help meet or mate, one who is call to help feel a need where there is a void, it is possible and healthy to give attention to your needs while assisting others. Make it a lifestyle habit to set aside time to focus solely on YOU. Learn the art of paying ATTENTION to YOU; this practice will eliminate and possibly prevent feelings of frustration, dissatisfaction, and resentment.

What does it mean to give attention to someone? Attention is defined as the capacity to maintain selective or sustained concentration;

observant care. Giving attention to your needs and desires is the state of consciously concentrating on you with care as you would do your spouse or child. I would arguably say that when we as women feel internally loved and outwardly appreciated for our acts of love the level of joy and peace exudes through our interactions with others.

So innocent but yet honest; I adore the transparency of a child. They are quick to express how they feel without apology. Could we learn something from a child's willingness to give attention to what they desire or need? I would say, "Absolutely!"

THE VISION, THE LETTER

As a creative thinker and woman who has a heart for seeing people win, a vision came to me several months ago that I believe will be an expression of love that empowers. I shared this vision with my god-mother who saw the need, as well as the impact that it could have on the lives of those who desire to embrace the art of loving themselves. Have you every purchased a card or written a letter to express your love and gratitude to someone on a special occasion? Allow me to introduce you to Unique Love Letters, a brand of love letters that are tailored and focused on you. The letter is unique because you are, and because this act of love is directed inwardly versus outwardly it is an uncommon and unique expression of love. www.UniqueLoveLetters.com

IT IS IN YOU

The power is IN you. "Now to Him (God) who is able to do exceedingly, abundantly, above all that we ask or think, according to the power that works IN us" (Ephesians 3:20). I repeat, "According to the POWER THAT WORKS IN US." It is IN you. Not loving, not believing in yourself will limit the power from working IN you. Whereas God loves us with an unconditional kind of love it is still our responsibility to grow to love ourselves. Growth comes through meditating in God's word and prayer, positive daily confessions, empowering versus debilitating associations, and actions of faith which stretches your potential and builds your confidence.

Take out the time to understand what you are carrying within; it will liberate you and those whom you associate with. Growth is not an event but a journey. Patiently embrace the journey, looking for an opportunity in every challenge. Life and all that it involves await your arrival because without your gift the void will remain where the need exist. I salute and celebrate you because you epitomize The Strength of a Woman.

The power is *IN* YOU.

God has turned your mess into a Masterpiece
For His glory!!!

I wrote a poem dedicated to women who are walking in the discovery of who they are. They have experienced feelings of loneliness, rejection, as well as power and impact. The poem is entitled "Love Me, Love Me Not" because at some point in life on the road of discovery we all have felt loved and unloved, even from ourselves. This poem is to you from me:

LOVE ME, LOVE ME NOT

Once upon a time I did not love me because I did not know me.
I partnered with failure, allowed defeat to move in;
Gossiped with fear and made excuses my best friend.
Inferiority was my nickname;
From low self-esteem and rejection I gained fame.
Did I love me? No! I loved me not.
Until I opened my heart and mind and realized I cannot be stopped.
If I would only trust God and believe that I can;
Who could stop me? Nothing, not even a man!
What is impossible with man is possible "with" God.
My mind has been renewed, my associations have changed;
I have chosen to live in my purpose and detach from all pain.
My head held high, no longer bowed in shame;
Failure, defeat, fear, and excuses are no longer a part of my name.
Inferiority, low self-esteem, and rejection are a thing of the past;
My voice shouts loudly, I AM FREE at last.
Free from the opinions of people, and the limitations that once held me back;
Free from internal confusion and all categories of lack.
I Am beautiful, gifted, and chosen to reign;
I Am a daughter of God, who He has called by name.
I Am Powerful! Yes, I now accept who I Am;
Love me? I Love me some me.
I have fallen in love with myself and God, and I am FREE.
Love me? Yes, I love me some me.

Prayer: Thank You Lord God for loving me even when I did not love myself. I am so grateful for the unconditional love that You extend toward me daily in spite my flaws. Father God I know that I am a work in progress, give me the grace and strength to fall in love with myself. Help me to love the person You made me to be without pretense. I declare this day that I love me and all that You created me to be. Amen!

What if you were giving the ability to see yourself through the eyes of God, what would you see?

_____
_____
_____
_____
_____
_____
_____
_____

Have you fallen in love with yourself? Explain.

_____
_____
_____
_____
_____
_____
_____
_____
_____
_____

Do you recognize the power that is housed within you? How can you effectively utilize that power on your behalf and the behalf of others?

_____
_____
_____
_____
_____
_____
_____
_____
_____
_____

What does it mean to give attention to you? Explain.

_____
_____
_____
_____
_____
_____
_____
_____
_____
_____

Notes

Unless otherwise identified definitions were retrieved from http://www.dictionary.com

Chapter 2 – The Enemy to Your Success

- Pastor Hart Ramsey uses Twitter (http://www.twitter.com/hartramsey)

Chapter 3 – Where is Your Trust?

- Pastor Michael D. Moore, Sermon, Faith Chapel Christian Center 2013

Chapter 4 – Positioned for Purpose

- Pastor Michael D. Moore, Sermon, Faith Chapel Christian Center 2013

Chapter 6 – Possess Your Power

- Pastor Michael D. Moore, sermon, Faith Chapel Christian Center 2012

Chapter 9 – Turn Your Passion into Profit

- Pastor Sherly Brady, public speech, TD Jakes Woman Thou Art Loosed conference Oct 2012

STAY CONNECTED

KINGDOM ENTREPRENEURS INTERNATIONAL Presents:

www.TheStrengthOfaWoman.com
www.YakineaMarie.com

FALL IN LOVE WITH YOURSELF

www.UniqueLoveLetters.com

IMPACT WOMEN'S BUSINESS & EMPOWERMENT NETWORK
www.LadiesofRoyalty.com

Believe God to the End

Made in the USA
Charleston, SC
16 September 2013